Pride & Prejudice

Jane Austen

retold by Jenny Dooley & Virginia Evans

Express Publishing

Published by Express Publishing
Liberty House, Greenham Business Park,
Newbury, Berkshire RG19 6HW
Tel: (0044) 1635 817 363 – Fax: (0044) 1635 817 463
e-mail: inquiries@expresspublishing.co.uk
http://www.expresspublishing.co.uk

© Jenny Dooley & Virginia Evans, 2012

Design & Illustration © Express Publishing, 2012

Colour Illustrations: Simon Andrews
© Express Publishing, 2012

Music composed and arranged by Peter Stone
© Express Publishing, 2012

First published 2012

Made in EU

ISBN 978-1-84862-945-5

Contents

Introduction 4

Chapter 1:   New Neighbours 8

Chapter 2:   Jane's Illness 16

Chapter 3:   Mr Collins and Mr Wickham 24

Chapter 4:   A Wedding 31

Chapter 5:   A Month in Kent 38

Chapter 6:   Darcy Opens his Heart 47

Chapter 7:   Pemberley 54

Chapter 8:   Disastrous News 61

Chapter 9:   Lydia's Way 68

Chapter 10:   Unexpected Endings 79

Activities: 90

Projects: 110

Word List: 114

Introductory Lesson

Before Reading

1. Look at the title of the book.
   a What does 'pride' mean?
   b What does 'prejudice' mean?
   c Can you think of any ways in which people can be proud or prejudiced?

Jane Austen

Jane Austen was born in Steventon, England, on 16th December 1775, the daughter of a clergyman, and one of eight children. She was tutored at home by her father, who encouraged her to write, and she wrote her first

2. 'Pride and Prejudice' is a novel of manners. Literary works of this kind deal with the social behaviour, habits and moral values of the people of a particular era. They often show a character's struggle to defy convention and social etiquette. What was the social context in Jane Austen's time like? Do you think it looks old-fashioned today?

3. Read Jane Austen's biography, then answer the questions:

   a When and where was Jane Austen born?
   b How many novels did she write?
   c What theme is important in her novels?
   d Where is she buried?
   e What are the typical features of her novels?

novel when she was only 14. Her greatest works were written later in her life. She finished six novels in all, including 'Sense and Sensibility' (1811), 'Pride and Prejudice' (1813) and 'Emma' (1816).

Even though marriage is an important theme in her novels, Jane Austen herself never married. She did receive a proposal when she was 27, but rejected it. The only man she judged worthy of marriage died before they could become engaged. Instead she continued to live a quiet life with her mother and her sister Cassandra, who was also unmarried. After a period of illness, Jane Austen died on 18th July 1817, and was buried in Winchester Cathedral.

Although her work received good reviews, her success during her lifetime was limited. Today she is regarded as one of the greatest novelists of the nineteenth century, and one of the greatest women writers of all time. Her work is best known for its realistic characters, her insights into the workings of relationships, and the irony with which she treats the attitudes of her times.

4) **Read the following statements. Circle 'True' or 'False'.**

1 Jane Austen had no support from her family when she started out as a writer.

   1 True   2 False

2 She wrote one of her gratest novels when she was a teenager.

   1 True   2 False

3 Jane Austen was against marriage.

   1 True   2 False

4 It was after her death that her books were considered great novels.

   1 True   2 False

5 Her books were written with a critical eye.

   1 True   2 False

Mr Bennet

Mrs Bennet

Jane Bennet

Mr Bin

Mr Wickham

Lydia Bennet

Mr Darcy

Elizabeth Bennet

Mr Collins

Charlotte Lucas

dy Catherine de Bourgh

Colonel Fitzwilliam

New Neighbours

*I*t is a truth universally acknowledged that a single man with a large fortune must be looking for a wife. And so, when such a wealthy young man moves into a neighbourhood, the local families hope that one of their daughters will soon be married to him.

One sunny autumn morning in their home at Longbourn, Mrs Bennet announced some important news.

"Have you heard that Netherfield Park has been let at last? It's a wonderful opportunity for our girls."

When Mr Bennet made no reply, Mrs Bennet continued.

"Don't you want to know who's taken it?"

Mr Bennet smiled ever so slightly as he responded to his wife.

"You want to tell me and I have no objection to hearing it."

"A wealthy single man by the name of Bingley is moving in."

"Really? How does it affect our girls?"

"Mr Bennet, you must know! I am hoping he will marry one of them! You should go and visit Mr Bingley as soon as he moves in."

"I don't think it's necessary for me to go. You and the girls can go, if you like."

"You know very well that we can't. Just think of what a marriage it would be for one of them. Even the Lucases are going and, as you know, they hardly ever go to welcome newcomers."

"I don't see why you can't go instead. I'll send Mr Bingley a note to give him my permission to marry whichever of them he chooses, although I must throw in a good word for my little Lizzy."

"You will do no such thing. Lizzy is no better than the others –

she's not as pretty as Jane or as outgoing as Lydia, and yet you always favour her."

"Well, they're all silly and ignorant, of course, but Lizzy is a little quicker to understand things than her sisters."

"Mr Bennet, how can you speak of your children like that? You so enjoy teasing me and have no concern for my nerves!"

Despite what he had said to his wife, Mr Bennet did visit Mr Bingley on the day after Mr Bingley moved in. That evening he decided to break the news to his family in his own way. He noticed Elizabeth repairing a hat.

"I hope Mr Bingley will like that hat, Lizzy."

Mrs Bennet responded before Lizzy could say a word.

"But, if we aren't going to visit Mr Bingley, how will he ever see Lizzy's hat?"

"You're forgetting, Mama, that we'll meet him at the public balls. Mrs Long has promised to introduce us."

Mr Bennet played along.

"When is your next ball, Lizzy?"

"There's one in Meryton in two weeks' time."

This worried Mrs Bennet.

"But Mrs Long will be away till the day before the ball. How can she introduce us, when she won't yet know him herself? Oh, I'm sick of Mr Bingley!"

Mr Bennet quite enjoyed the next moment.

"I'm sorry to hear that. If you had told me, I wouldn't have visited him this morning. Now, we cannot simply ignore him."

Mrs Bennet and her daughters' concern turned to joy. Mr Bingley was certain to be at the ball in Meryton!

Mrs Bennet and her five daughters had arrived early at the assembly rooms in Meryton. They were all eagerly awaiting the arrival of Mr Bingley and his party. At last they came – Mr Bingley, his two sisters and two other men. Mr Bingley was a friendly young man, and everyone found him pleasant. His sisters were very stylishly dressed – more so than any of the other women in the hall. One of the other men was Mr Hurst, who was married to one of the sisters. But it was Mr Darcy who attracted the most attention. He was tall and handsome, and rumours quickly spread that he was very wealthy. But people noticed his pride most of all. He did not want to meet any of the ladies and danced only two dances – one with each of Mr Bingley's sisters.

Elizabeth Bennet watched Mr Bingley's party from a distance. She enjoyed studying people and trying to make out their characters. Later, when she was talking with her older sister Jane, Mr Bingley came up to be introduced. Now she found herself seated on her own, watching as Bingley danced with Jane. When the dance finished, Mr Bingley came to talk with Mr Darcy, who was standing close by. Elizabeth knew they were talking about her, and felt her heart pounding.

"Come, Darcy, why aren't you dancing?"

"You know I dance only with women I know."

"But there are several very pretty women here."

"You are dancing with the only pretty girl in the place, Bingley."

"Jane is very beautiful, but one of her sisters is just over there."

"She's tolerable, I suppose, but not pretty enough to tempt me."

From that moment Elizabeth disliked Mr Darcy.

The rest of the evening passed pleasantly. Mrs Bennet was very happy that Mr Bingley had danced with her eldest daughter and that his sisters thought well of her. Jane herself was pleased about this, and Elizabeth was happy for her. Lydia and Catherine were excited to have danced all night. Mary had overheard someone praising her, so they all returned to Longbourn in good spirits.

The following day Jane was still very excited, and could not wait to tell Elizabeth all about her evening.

"Mr Bingley is such a nice man, don't you think, Lizzy?"

"He certainly is, and handsome!"

"He's just what a man should be. He's outgoing, has a good sense of humour, and he asked me to dance with him twice! Such a compliment! I can hardly believe it!"

"A compliment maybe, but one you deserved."

Of the many things that were said about the ball, some things were generally agreed upon, Elizabeth realised. Certainly Mr Bingley was well-liked by everyone, and his interest in Jane had been well received. Elizabeth would not be surprised if her beautiful sister found a husband and someone as well thought of as Mr Bingley.

Opinions differed more about Mr Bingley's sisters, Mrs Hurst and Miss Bingley. They were clearly well-dressed, well-mannered and well-educated, and Jane thought highly of them. But to Elizabeth they had seemed proud and self-important.

Everyone seemed to agree that Mr Darcy was full of pride. And even though he had good looks and wealth, Elizabeth promised herself that she would never dance with him, even if he asked her. She neither knew nor cared that Darcy was quite taken by her light figure and dark eyes.

But Elizabeth wondered what the future would be for Bingley and Jane. In the days that followed, they saw each other quite often, although only in the company of others. Bingley's sisters liked Jane, too, so maybe something would come of it. She hoped so because she could see that her sister was falling in love.

Jane's Illness

A couple of weeks after the ball, Jane Bennet received a note from Miss Bingley. She was inviting Jane to have dinner with her and her sister, Mrs Hurst, at Netherfield that evening. Jane was very happy to get an invitation from such important neighbours, even though Mr Bingley would be out and she would not see him.

Mrs Bennet insisted that Jane go on horseback. It looked like rain and, if the weather turned bad, she would have to stay overnight. Then she would most likely see Mr Bingley the next morning. The plan worked, and Jane did not return to Longbourn that night.

The next morning, the Bennets received a note saying that Jane was ill, probably due to the weather, and would be staying at Netherfield until she was better.

The note worried Elizabeth and she set off straight away on foot through the muddy fields to Netherfield.

When she arrived, Miss Bingley and Mrs Hurst were shocked that she had walked so far, and Elizabeth had the feeling that they disapproved of her.

"How is Jane?"

Miss Bingley responded coolly.

"She's got a fever and is not well enough to leave her room."

The doctor called at the house a little later, and told Jane to stay in bed. Elizabeth, Miss Bingley and Mrs Hurst sat by her bedside and kept her company. At three o'clock, Elizabeth said it was time for her to leave, and Miss Bingley offered to send for the carriage.

Jane seemed disappointed, so Miss Bingley invited Elizabeth to stay until her sister was completely well. Elizabeth gratefully

accepted the offer. She sent word to Longbourn to inform her family and ask them to send fresh clothes.

That evening, Mr Bingley and Mr Darcy returned to Netherfield just in time for dinner. Darcy said little, but Bingley was very concerned about Jane's condition. Though Miss Bingley and Mrs Hurst asked after Jane's health, Elizabeth noticed that they were rather unconcerned about her sister when she was not present. Bingley's genuine concern, however, pleased her very much.

After dinner, Elizabeth returned to Jane. Almost as soon as Elizabeth had left the room, Miss Bingley began to criticise her.

"Did you see the state she was in when she arrived here? The mud must have been six inches deep on her clothes."

Mrs Hurst agreed.

"Dirty clothes, messy hair – I don't know why she came at all."

But Mr Bingley saw it differently.

"I think it shows that she really cares for her sister, to come all that way on foot."

Mrs Hurst then shifted her remarks to Jane.

"I have a high regard for Miss Jane Bennet, she is really a very sweet girl. I hope she soon finds a good husband, but her chances must be poor, with the kind of family she comes from and their lack of status."

Again, Mr Bingley defended the Bennet sisters.

"Whatever you say of their family, it doesn't make them any less good company."

Darcy then remarked on the situation.

"But their family will certainly make it harder for them to find good husbands."

Bingley said nothing, but Miss Bingley and Mrs Hurst seemed very pleased at Darcy's remark.

The next day, Jane was no better, and Elizabeth asked that Mrs Bennet come to visit. Naturally, Mrs Bennet wanted Jane to remain at Netherfield for as long as possible. She hoped that her daughter's nearness to Mr Bingley would increase the chances of a marriage between them. She opened the conversation.

"You have a beautiful home, Mr Bingley."

"Thank you. I like living here."

As always, Elizabeth was observing human nature.

"I think this house is in line with your personality."

"Really? So you're a student of character?"

"I am. I enjoy trying to work out what makes someone the way they are."

Mr Darcy then offered his own opinion about country living.

"But in the country you don't meet many different people to study. Certainly not as many people as you do in town."

"Maybe not, but people change over time and there's always something new to see in them."

Mrs Bennet was displeased by Mr Darcy's remarks about country life.

"I quite assure you that there's just as much going on in the country as there is in town."

Everyone was surprised, and Darcy, after looking at Mrs Bennet for a moment, turned silently away. Mrs Bennet sensed a victory.

"The town's only advantage is its shops and public places. The country is much more beautiful, isn't it, Mr Bingley?"

"When I'm here in the country, I want to stay here, but when I'm in town, I want to stay there. I like them both."

"You're not like Mr Darcy, then, for he sees nothing of value in the country."

Her mother's remark made Elizabeth feel very uncomfortable.

"Mama, you're mistaken, Mr Darcy only said that there is a greater variety of people in town. You can't disagree with that."

"Of course, my dear, but this part of the countryside also has a great many people. Why, we dine with four and twenty different families!"

This statement, having little to do with the truth, left Elizabeth blushing and she quickly changed the subject. Mrs Bennet, however, failed to see the stupidity of her remarks and for the next half hour she continued to embarrass everyone. When she finally left, it was a great relief to them all.

That evening, Miss Bingley and her sister entertained the others by playing the piano. Elizabeth noticed that Mr Darcy often looked at her. But she put the possibility out of her mind that such a man would be attracted to her, especially after what he had said at the Meryton ball. So why he might look at her so much, she had little idea. However, since she did not care at all for him, it did not really matter whether he looked at her or not.

After some Italian songs, Miss Bingley started playing lively Scottish music. At this point, Mr Darcy stood and came over to where Elizabeth was sitting.

"Are you tempted to dance, Miss Bennet?"

She smiled, but made no answer. He repeated the question, a little surprised by her silence.

"I heard you before, but I couldn't decide what to say. I know you wanted me to say 'Yes', but only so that you could have made fun of me for having such bad taste. And so I'll say 'No' to your question – look down on me if you dare!"

"Indeed, I do not dare."

Darcy then calmly returned to where he had been sitting. It surprised Elizabeth that he was not annoyed when she refused to dance with him.

The next day, Jane began to feel a lot better. Miss Bingley and Mrs Hurst joined Elizabeth once more at Jane's bedside, and they talked until dinner. After dinner, they stayed downstairs, leaving Jane to sleep.

When the gentlemen entered the room, Miss Bingley started to pay Mr Darcy a lot of attention. But Darcy was not interested, and chose to write a letter to his sister.

Miss Bingley then walked about the room and tried to attract Darcy's attention, but he did not look up from his letter. So she turned to Elizabeth for help.

"Miss Eliza Bennet, would you like to join me for a walk round the room?"

Elizabeth was surprised, but agreed. Now that Elizabeth was walking too, Darcy looked up and Miss Bingley took the opportunity to speak.

"Would you like to join us, Mr Darcy?"

"No, there could be only two reasons why you two might choose to walk round the room. And for either of these two reasons I would be interfering if I joined you, Miss Bingley."

"Whatever do you mean?"

"Well, you might be walking about the room because you want a private conversation with each other. In that case my presence would intrude on your privacy. Or, you might want to show off your figure. In that case I have a far better view from here."

"Really! I never heard anything so shameful!"

Miss Bingley turned to Elizabeth.

"What shall we do to punish him?"

"I think we should make fun of him."

"In what way?"

Elizabeth pretended to think for a moment.

"Well, that's a difficult matter. We must find a fault in his character, and pick on that. But perhaps there are no faults in his character."

Darcy was almost amused.

"I think you're flattering me. I try hard to hide any faults that might make someone laugh at me."

"Such as vanity and pride?"

"Yes, vanity is a fault. But pride is different. If the mind is superior, then pride can be hidden."

At this reply, Elizabeth turned away to hide a smile, and Miss Bingley asked her final opinion on the matter.

"So, Miss Bennet, what is your decision?"

"I'm totally convinced that Mr Darcy has no faults."

"I have many faults. For example, once my good opinion of someone is lost, it is lost forever."

Elizabeth could not hold back.

"That is a weakness indeed! To be so unforgiving is a major fault. But you have chosen your fault well. I really cannot laugh at it."

Darcy was ready with a reply.

"Nobody is perfect."

Elizabeth shot back a response of her own.

"And your fault is to hate everybody."

"And your fault is to wilfully misunderstand them."

Miss Bingley was now tired of a conversation from which she had been left out.

"Do let us have some music!"

The next day, Jane was well enough to travel, and she and Elizabeth returned home to Longbourn.

Mr Collins and Mr Wickham

The next day, Mr Bennet told the family of a letter he had received from a cousin, Mr Collins. Mr Collins had requested to come and stay with them for a week. He was the only other male in all the Bennet family and so was to inherit Longbourn after Mr Bennet's death. Mr Collins was a priest who lived in Kent, and none of the Bennet family had ever met him before. His letter was a strange one, as it was full of apologies and expressions of discomfort regarding the Longbourn inheritance situation. It also spoke in several places in the most radiant terms of his patroness, Lady Catherine de Bourgh. The Bennet family therefore expected a slightly strange man.

When Mr Collins arrived, he did indeed fulfil these expectations. His conversation was clumsy and he apologised often for his unintended insults.

The Bennets later learnt the reason for his visit. On the suggestion of Lady Catherine, Mr Collins was looking for a wife, and he had decided to find one amongst the Bennet girls. It was his idea of making amends for inheriting their father's estate and he had heard of their beauty.

He was particularly attracted by Jane's beauty. However, Mrs Bennet told him that Jane was "likely to be very soon engaged", and so he switched his attentions to Elizabeth. Mrs Bennet, now realising Mr Collins' marriage intentions, did everything she could to encourage him. But Elizabeth did not at first realise what was going on.

The next evening, there was a dinner at Mrs Philips' house. Mrs Philips was Elizabeth's aunt who lived in Meryton. All the

girls were to go, along with Mr Collins. But the younger two, Lydia and Kitty, were especially interested in meeting the army officers who would be there. A regiment had set up camp near Meryton, and they often saw the red-coated soldiers in the streets. Lydia, in particular, was taken with the men in uniform.

For Elizabeth, the evening was notable for a long conversation with one of these officers, a Mr Wickham. It was after dinner had finished, and everyone else had been drawn to the card tables. But Wickham and Elizabeth sat alone. In the conversation, Netherfield was mentioned and Elizabeth discovered that Wickham knew Mr Darcy. Wickham inquired as to the length of Darcy's stay and whether Elizabeth knew him well.

"He's been there about a month and I know him as much as I ever wish to. I've spent four days in the same house with him, and I don't like him at all."

Wickham declared that he, too, was not fond of Darcy.

"I grew up with him, but I don't get on well with him either, although his father, the late Mr Darcy, was the most wonderful man I have ever met. Mr Darcy paid for me to train to become a priest, but when he died, Darcy went against his father's wishes and prevented me from taking up my intended post. I was left no choice but to join the army."

"That's shocking! Darcy deserves to be publicly disgraced!"

"Yes, and one day he will be. But not by me – I cannot easily forget the kindness of his father. The hardest thing for me to bear is that I never did anything wrong."

"But why did he behave so cruelly?"

Wickham had an answer ready.

"I think it comes down to jealousy, or maybe it's simply pride."

Elizabeth heartily agreed.

"Pride – yes, everyone thinks that he's proud."

"Maybe he couldn't bear the thought of my having something granted by his father."

Elizabeth was horrified by this story. She had never imagined that Darcy could have done what Wickham had told her. But the story certainly confirmed her own impression of him, that Darcy was not the sort of man she wanted to associate with.

Wickham and Elizabeth went on talking for most of the evening. They talked about Meryton and its people, and the area. Elizabeth found him very charming, and was looking forward to meeting him again.

A ball was to be held at Netherfield in two days' time, and Mr Bingley had invited all the officers. It turned out to be a magnificent event. But all its magnificence was of little concern to Elizabeth. She searched for Wickham amongst the guests, but he was nowhere to be seen. At last she discovered that he had had to go to London on business, and would not be attending the ball.

She had not got over the disappointment of Wickham's absence when the dancing began. Suddenly, Mr Darcy came up to her and asked her to dance. Caught off guard, she agreed, and found herself dancing with a man she disliked greatly. For a while they danced in silence, but then Elizabeth decided that she would speak.

"I met an old friend of yours, a Mr Wickham. A very nice gentleman."

Elizabeth's respect for Wickham concerned Mr Darcy.

"Mr Wickham has indeed got a pleasant manner that ensures he makes many friends, but he has a problem keeping them."

"He certainly has lost your friendship, and that has proven very costly for him."

At this, Darcy became noticeably uncomfortable. They finished the dance in silence.

Only a few minutes after the dance had ended, Miss Bingley came up to Elizabeth.

"I hear that you've met Mr Wickham and that he has been telling you stories. I have no doubt that anything he said was highly critical of Mr Darcy, but I can tell you myself that Mr Darcy is a fine and honest person."

Elizabeth did not believe Miss Bingley. For Elizabeth, Darcy's pride was noticeable in everything he said, and anyone so proud was likely to have unpleasant relationships with others. So it was very easy for her to believe what Wickham had said.

Later Elizabeth went to find Jane to see if she knew anything about Wickham.

Jane's response favoured Darcy.

"Mr Bingley hasn't heard the whole of the story, but he has no doubt that Darcy has not done anything wrong."

Elizabeth pursued the notion further.

"Does Bingley know Wickham personally?"

"No."

"So Bingley's version of the situation must have come from Darcy. I'm sure Mr Bingley is being totally honest about what he knows. But since he knows only what Darcy has told him, I've no doubt that it is not totally truthful."

It all made total sense to Elizabeth. She was convinced that Darcy had wronged Wickham in a shameful way.

A Wedding

*B*efore breakfast the next day, Mr Collins made his move. Seeing Mrs Bennet with Elizabeth and Kitty, he approached them.

"Mrs Bennet, would you mind if I had a private word with Elizabeth?"

"Yes, of course. Come on, Kitty, we have to go upstairs."

As soon as Mrs Bennet and Kitty had gone, Mr Collins began. He spent several minutes explaining to Elizabeth that he was now at the time of life when he needed a wife. Since he had established himself in a profession and had a nice home in Kent which needed looking after, he thought he must look for a wife immediately. He boldly expected a positive response.

"You'll be very happy there."

"I think you're being a little hasty, Mr Collins. Thank you for your offer, but I'm afraid it's impossible for me to accept."

"Come now, I know it's the custom for you young ladies to refuse the first offer, but just think what it is you're turning down."

"I have thought about it as long as I need, Mr Collins, and thinking about it more will not make it any more attractive."

But for several more minutes Mr Collins tried to persuade her, until finally she left him to go to her room. Ten minutes later, Elizabeth was summoned to the library to speak with her father.

"Lizzy, tell me, I understand that Mr Collins has proposed to you. Is that true?"

She nodded.

"And you refused him?"

"Yes."

"Very well. We now come to the point. Your mother insists upon you accepting it, don't you, Mrs Bennet?"

"Yes, or I will never see her again."

"This leaves you with an unfortunate choice. Your mother will never see you again if you do not marry Mr Collins, and I will never see you again if you do."

Elizabeth could not help smiling, but her mother was beside herself, and complained bitterly for a long time. She tried to persuade Elizabeth to change her mind, but without success.

Later that morning, Charlotte Lucas, Elizabeth's best friend, arrived to spend the day at Longbourn. Lydia rushed out to tell her the news.

"I'm glad you came, because there's been so much fun going on here. Mr Collins proposed to Elizabeth, but she won't have him!"

In the breakfast room, Mrs Bennet put her side of the matter to Charlotte.

"You must convince her. No one is on my side. No one feels for my poor nerves!"

At that moment Elizabeth and Jane entered the room, and Mrs Bennet went on.

"Ah, here she is! Completely carefree and unconcerned! But I'm telling you, Miss Lizzy, if you carry on refusing every marriage proposal you get, you'll never find a husband. And I won't be able to support you once my husband is dead!"

Mrs Bennet carried on in this way until Mr Collins came in. Mr Collins' pride was hurt by Elizabeth's rejection, but not his feelings, as he never was in love with her. He handled the situation by refusing to speak to her for the rest of his stay. Fortunately for everyone, Charlotte engaged him in lengthy conversation, drawing his attention away from the situation, and Longbourn became more peaceful.

The next day a letter arrived for Jane. It was from Miss Bingley. Jane read it out to Elizabeth.

"She says that they're all leaving Netherfield for the winter. Mr Bingley had to go straight away to London, and…"

"So suddenly?"

"Oh, Lizzy, I won't see him for the whole winter!"

Jane turned back to the letter. Suddenly her face dropped.

"There's more. She says that she has good reason to believe that Mr Bingley is interested in Georgiana, Mr Darcy's sister."

Elizabeth thought for a moment and then gave her sister her opinion.

"I think Miss Bingley sees that her brother is in love with you, but she wants him to marry Miss Darcy instead. She will probably follow him to London in the hope of keeping him there, and try to persuade you that he does not care about you."

"Miss Bingley would never try to deceive me like that!"

Elizabeth had her own ideas.

"Perhaps then she is deceiving herself."

Nevertheless, there was no doubt that Bingley was leaving Netherfield for the winter. This alone was disastrous news for Jane, and for many days she could not be comforted.

The same day the letter arrived, the Bennets and Mr Collins went to visit the Lucases. Once again, Charlotte Lucas spent most of the day talking to Mr Collins. Elizabeth was grateful that her friend had occupied him and thanked her for it. But for Charlotte, there was more at stake than merely keeping Mr Collins happy or keeping his attention away from Elizabeth. She was actually trying to redirect Mr Collins' attentions onto herself. Indeed, her scheme was working well, and if he weren't leaving Hertfordshire so soon, she felt certain she would succeed.

The next morning, Mr Collins sneaked out of Longbourn soon after dawn, and walked towards the Lucases' house, for he had a similar scheme. Charlotte saw him approaching from an upstairs window, and rushed outside to intercept him in the lane.

There, in the shortest speech that Mr Collins had ever made, they became engaged. On returning to the house, Charlotte's parents swiftly and joyfully gave their consent to the marriage.

It came as a complete surprise to Elizabeth that her friend would accept Mr Collins's proposal, and she demanded an explanation when Charlotte told her about the engagement.

"How could you?"

"Well, I hope that in time you'll come to understand why I did it. I've never been a romantic, and Mr Collins is offering me a comfortable life. I think I have a very good chance of being happy."

Elizabeth was filled with disbelief. Just three days after Mr Collins had proposed to her, he had proposed to someone else! But her surprise at this was nothing compared to her amazement that Charlotte could consider marrying purely for money, and she wondered if their friendship could ever be the same. She also felt sad in her certainty that her friend would never be happy in the life she had chosen.

The days came and went. Elizabeth saw a lot of Mr Wickham, and enjoyed his company. Jane tried not to show it but she was broken-hearted over Mr Bingley.

As Christmas approached, Elizabeth's aunt and uncle, Mr and Mrs Gardiner from London, came to stay at Longbourn. Elizabeth had always had a good relationship with Mrs Gardiner, and confided in her all her hopes and concerns about Jane and Mr Bingley. Mrs Gardiner suggested that Jane come and stay with her after their visit to help her get over him. She also thought that Elizabeth's

relationship with Wickham was highly unlikely to come to anything, and advised her not to encourage him and to see him less often. After considering her aunt's point of view, Elizabeth could see the sense in it and took her advice. Mrs Gardiner also suggested to Elizabeth that she go with them to Derbyshire in the summer. Elizabeth agreed immediately.

In January, not long after the Gardiners had returned to London, Mr Collins returned to Hertfordshire for his wedding. After the wedding, he and Charlotte would live at his home in Hunsford in Kent. Charlotte invited Elizabeth to come to stay with them for a visit in March. She accepted the invitation, although she doubted that it would be particularly enjoyable. She felt that she and Charlotte would never be the close friends they used to be.

As the weeks passed, the visit to Kent looked more attractive to Elizabeth, especially when she discovered that Mr Wickham had become very interested in another young woman. This woman, a Miss King, had the enormous advantage of having a dowry worth £10,000. Elizabeth could not compete with such wealth. If nothing else, Elizabeth was now certain that Wickham had no interest in marrying her and she did not think ill of either him or Miss King.

Jane had returned with her aunt and uncle to London and wrote to Elizabeth regularly. She had seen Miss Bingley only once in the last month and found her cool and distant. She had not seen Mr Bingley at all, and Elizabeth suspected that his sister had not informed him that Jane was in town.

A Month in Kent

*I*n March, as planned, Elizabeth went to stay with Charlotte and her new husband in Hunsford in Kent. When she arrived at the parsonage, she was greeted warmly by both. She was shown round the house, and then they took a walk in the extensive gardens.

As they walked, Mr Collins had some news to announce.

"We have all been invited to go to Rosings tomorrow evening."

Rosings was Lady Catherine de Bourgh's nearby estate. Mr Collins went on about Lady Catherine's fine qualities.

"It will be a privilege which I'm sure you'll enjoy. Lady Catherine truly is a remarkable lady. In fact we dine there twice a week."

Lady Catherine's home was the largest and grandest that Elizabeth had ever seen, and the dinner matched the house in its elegance and proportion. Lady Catherine talked a lot, and about a great variety of things. She asked Elizabeth numerous questions about her family and her background, and asked Charlotte to tell her everything that was happening in her life. Lady Catherine's daughter, Anne, was very quiet. She was about fifteen, but was very small and thin for her age and appeared pale and sickly.

Elizabeth found two things about that evening disturbing. The first was Lady Catherine's insistence upon knowing her age, which Elizabeth was very reluctant to say. But Lady Catherine was not someone who people normally stood up to, and Elizabeth finally told her.

The second was her discovery that Mr Darcy was Lady Catherine's nephew. Lady Catherine spoke well of him and it was not too

surprising to Elizabeth when Lady Catherine added that Mr Darcy would soon marry her daughter. But when Elizabeth looked at Anne, and saw a very weak and ill child, she doubted that Anne would be the sort of wife that Darcy would want to have. But Lady Catherine seemed certain that it would happen, saying that Darcy and Anne were 'destined to marry'.

It was not long before Darcy came. He did not come alone, however, but with his cousin, Colonel Fitzwilliam.

As the evening progressed, it became clear that she much preferred to talk with her nephews, and especially Darcy. Elizabeth found herself talking with Fitzwilliam, and it was indeed a very pleasant conversation. In fact, after a while it attracted Lady Catherine's attention.

"What are you talking about to Miss Bennet, Fitzwilliam? Let me hear what it is."

"We're talking about music, madam."

"About music! Then let's hear it. There are few people in England, I suppose, who have more true enjoyment of music than I, or a better natural taste. If I'd ever learnt, I would have been an expert pianist."

Colonel Fitzwilliam responded agreeably.

"I don't doubt it! Meanwhile, I've managed to persuade Miss Bennet to play for us."

Elizabeth went to the piano and started to play. Darcy approached the piano and stood so he had a clear view of Elizabeth's face. Elizabeth smiled and addressed him.

"Do you mean to frighten me, Mr Darcy? I can be very stubborn when put in such situations, and my courage rises when I'm being bullied."

"I won't say that you're mistaken because I know you don't really think I'm trying to bully you. And I've known you long enough to know that you often like to express opinions which in fact are not your own."

Elizabeth laughed at this description of herself. Then she turned to Colonel Fitzwilliam.

"I see your cousin has an unkind notion of me, and will teach you not to believe a word I say. And Mr Darcy, I don't think it's very nice to mention what you learnt of my character in Hertfordshire. It is also unwise, since I might retaliate and say something that will shock your relations."

Darcy smiled.

"I'm not afraid of you."

Colonel Fitzwilliam joined in.

"I think you should tell us what you know of him. I'd like to know how he behaves with others."

"Well, prepare yourself to hear something dreadful. The first time I saw Mr Darcy was at a ball, and there he danced only two times all night, even though there were far more ladies than gentlemen."

Darcy was quick to defend himself.

"I did not know anyone but my own small party."

"True, but you could have been introduced."

"Perhaps you are right but I feel uncomfortable meeting new people."

Neither Elizabeth nor Fitzwilliam was going to let him get away with an easy answer.

"Shall we ask your cousin the reason for this?"

"I can tell you myself. He simply can't be bothered to make the effort it requires."

Darcy again came to his own defence.

"I'm not as able as others to talk easily with people I have never met before."

Elizabeth's reply was quick and clever.

"Perhaps, but my fingers do not play this piano with the same expert manner as many other women do. I lack the skill to play quickly or with great expression. I've always thought this was my own fault because I do not practise enough, and not because I lack the ability to play better."

Mr Darcy smiled.

"You're quite right, of course. Neither of us performs for strangers."

But at this point their conversation was interrupted by Lady Catherine. Again, she was curious as to the topic of conversation and wanted to know why Elizabeth had stopped playing. Elizabeth immediately started playing again, and Lady Catherine came closer.

"Miss Bennet plays well, but she would play much better if she practised more."

Over the next few days, Elizabeth saw a lot of Mr Darcy and his relations. One morning, when she was out for a walk alone, Elizabeth ran into Colonel Fitzwilliam. Since they were both heading to the parsonage, they walked together and chatted. Elizabeth spoke first.

"You're leaving on Saturday, I hear."

"Yes – if Darcy doesn't put it off again."

"I imagine Darcy brought you here mainly to have some company. I'm surprised he doesn't marry, because then he would have constant companionship. But perhaps his sister is good enough company for the time being and, as she's under his sole care, he can tell her what to do."

Colonel Fitzwilliam clarified a point for Elizabeth.

"Actually, I have joint responsibility with him for his sister."

"Do you really? Tell me, is she difficult? Sixteen is a difficult age, and if she has the true Darcy spirit, she may like to have her own way."

Fitzwilliam looked at her intensely, in a way which suggested to Elizabeth that Georgiana was indeed difficult to manage, but she reassured him.

"You needn't worry; I've not heard anything about Miss Darcy misbehaving. In fact, I've heard only good things."

"Darcy takes good care of her, as he does with all his friends."

Elizabeth was a little surprised.

"Does he really? And the same for all his friends?"

"Yes. For example, a few days ago he told me that he had saved one of his friends from an unwise marriage."

"Really? Did he say why he thought the marriage unwise?"

"All he said was that there were some strong objections towards the lady."

Elizabeth's thoughts turned suddenly to Mr Bingley, and this raised her curiosity.

"Did he say which friend?"

"No, though I thought it might have been Bingley. It's the kind of mistake Bingley would make."

When Elizabeth had time to reflect on this conversation, she concluded that it was very likely that this friend Darcy had saved was indeed Bingley, and that the lady from whom Bingley had been 'saved' must have been Jane. If this were the case, then she was right in thinking Bingley had wanted to marry Jane, but now it seemed that the only thing that had prevented his proposing was Darcy's advice. But what objections could Darcy possibly raise against Jane? They could only be, Elizabeth thought, to do with her family, and its lack of wealth and connections.

Then she remembered the letter that Miss Bingley had sent to

Jane, which had claimed that her brother was attracted to Miss Darcy. Perhaps this gave Darcy another reason for stopping Bingley from proposing to Jane, one that had nothing to do with her. Perhaps Darcy merely wanted Bingley to marry his sister. She decided that Darcy must have acted partly out of the worst kind of pride and partly out of the wish to keep Bingley for his sister. These thoughts angered Elizabeth greatly, and her opinion of Mr Darcy worsened.

Darcy Opens his Heart

*E*lizabeth's conversation with Colonel Fitzwilliam had left her a little shaken. Although that afternoon she and Charlotte and Mr Collins had been invited to go to Rosings for tea, she did not feel up to it. It was partly the thought of having to see Darcy and knowing now that it was he who had convinced Bingley not to marry Jane. She developed a headache, so she stayed at the parsonage alone.

When the doorbell rang, a couple of hours later, Elizabeth thought it might be Colonel Fitzwilliam, come to see if she were better. She was wrong. It was Darcy. She just stood there in amazement as he strode into the drawing room of the parsonage.

"They said that you were unwell. Are you any better?"

"A little better, thank you."

Darcy sat down, said nothing, then after half a minute stood again, and walked around the room. Elizabeth did not know what to say. There were often silences when they were alone together, but this time he seemed particularly nervous. Finally he spoke.

"I have struggled against my feelings but they won't go away. I must tell you how passionately I love you."

She was speechless. She just stared at him, not entirely certain that she had heard him correctly.

"I know there's a real difference between the wealth of my family and yours, and I know that my feelings for you seem to go against all reason, but they are real nonetheless. I have done everything in my power but my feelings for you are so strong that they have completely got the better of me. I hope they will now be rewarded by your hand in marriage."

Elizabeth felt herself blushing. She knew of course that she would never accept his proposal, but for a moment she felt sorry for him, since she knew the pain of rejection would be great. However, as he continued to talk of how he loved her despite her lower social standings and the shame it would bring him, she became angry.

"If I felt grateful, I should thank you for the compliment, but I cannot. I have never wanted your attention, and I do not want to marry you."

Darcy, of course, resented her rejection.

"And is this all you are going to say? Why do you refuse me so rudely?"

"Why did you choose to tell me that you love me against your will, against all reason? That was hardly a compliment. And how could you ever think I would accept a man who has ruined my sister's chances of happiness, perhaps forever? Or do you deny that you had anything to do with that?"

"I do not deny it. I think it was the right thing to do, and saved Bingley from an unfortunate mistake. I helped him but could not help myself."

"But it is not only this that makes me dislike you. What you did to Mr Wickham is shameful. You've ruined the best years of his life, and denied him his independence!"

Darcy now strode around the room.

"So this is your opinion of me! Thank you for explaining it so fully! Perhaps my honesty about how I tried not to love you has offended you."

"You are mistaken, Mr Darcy. Even if you had behaved more like a gentleman just now, I would still have refused. From the very first time I met you, you have been proud and high-handed beyond belief. You clearly don't care about the feelings of others.

In fact, I had not known you a month before I felt you were the last man in the world I would ever marry!"

Darcy had now stopped striding. He appeared surprised at her words.

"Thank you, you've been very clear about your feelings. I won't take up any more of your time."

And with that he turned and strode towards the door and left the house. Then Elizabeth sat down exhausted and cried for half an hour.

The next morning, Elizabeth went for her usual walk. This time she had much to think about. A marriage proposal from Darcy! She was still amazed.

Suddenly she heard her name being called. She turned. It was Darcy! She started walking away, but he caught up with her, and thrust a letter towards her.

"Please read this. I can assure you that Colonel Fitzwilliam can back up everything I have written."

Instinctively she took it. As soon as he was out of sight, Elizabeth opened the letter. She was curious, but did not expect to enjoy whatever was written within.

"Dear Miss Bennet,

Do not be alarmed by this letter. I do not intend to hurt you or embarrass myself by repeating anything that was said last night. There were two accusations that you made for which I wish to explain my actions and my motives.

The first concerns my advice to Bingley not to propose to your sister, Jane. I first became aware of the closeness of their relationship at the Netherfield ball. I watched them closely that evening, and noticed that, although your sister seemed to enjoy Bingley's company, she was also holding something back. My conclusion was that she did not really care for him. However, from what you said to me yesterday, I must have been wrong.

I also believed that your family, if I may be so bold, was a problem. In terms of wealth and social standing, it is of course much lower than Bingley's, but there is also the matter of the embarrassing behaviour of your mother and your younger sisters.

As a result of these concerns, I advised Bingley that marrying your sister would not be in his best interests and convinced him that she did not feel as deeply for him as he did for her. My only other involvement in this matter was that I did not tell him that I knew your sister was in London. I admit this was low of me but it was done with the best intention, out of friendship. If I hurt your sister's feelings, I did not know it.

Your second accusation, that I have mistreated Mr Wickham, is unfair. But I will tell you the facts so that you can judge for yourself. After my father died about five years ago, Mr Wickham told me that he had decided against a career in the church, and had decided to study law instead. He asked me for money to support him, and I gave him £3,000. But it turned out that he never studied at all, and lived a life of excess and laziness. Three years later he asked for more money when he had used up all his money on high living, but I refused him.

Last year, though, he managed to win the affection of my sister, Georgiana, when she was being educated in London. She was only fifteen, but he convinced her to elope with him. Fortunately, she told me about her plans two days before, and of course I swiftly put an end to them. I have no doubt that all he wanted was her money and revenge on me. Wickham had a lot to gain of course, since my sister has a large fortune of £30,000. I hope you will keep all of this to yourself, since I am sure you can imagine the kind of damage it might cause my sister and me."

She folded up the letter and decided not to look at it again.

But two minutes later, she opened the letter again and started to re-read it. She considered again what Darcy said about Wickham. If it was true, then Darcy had done little wrong. The very fact that Darcy had said that Colonel Fitzwilliam would back up everything in the letter made her think he may be telling the truth. She recalled the evening she had talked with Wickham. Now something occurred to her that she had not thought of before. What Wickham had told her now seemed too personal to tell a total stranger, as she had been to him then. That made Wickham's whole account suspicious. But also, Wickham's recent involvement with Miss King began to appear suspicious – perhaps he was concerned only with getting his hands on her money, and didn't care for her at all.

So, Elizabeth thought to herself,

"I've been so prejudiced against Mr Darcy and for Wickham. I missed signs that would have revealed Wickham's dishonesty!"

She felt ashamed of herself.

With a changed attitude, she read again the part of the letter in which Darcy discussed Jane. She understood that Jane did tend to conceal her feelings, more than most people. Indeed, it might well be possible that someone like Darcy, who did not know Jane well, would fail to recognise the strong feelings she had for Bingley.

When Elizabeth finally returned to the parsonage, over two hours later, her opinion of Darcy had changed greatly.

She found that both Mr Darcy and Colonel Fitzwilliam had called while she was out and had now left Rosings.

Pemberley

A few days later, Elizabeth returned to Longbourn. After all that had happened in Kent, she was glad to be home.

Lydia told her some news within minutes of her return. The regiment was leaving Meryton, and was going to Brighton. They were going in two weeks' time. For Lydia this was quite the worst news imaginable – what would she do without any officers to talk or dream about?

"Kitty and I are trying to persuade our father to take us to Brighton for the summer."

Elizabeth, however, was far from displeased.

"Really?"

But Lydia had more news. It concerned their friend, Mr Wickham. "There is no danger of his marrying Mary King after all. She has gone to stay with her uncle in Liverpool. He is safe."

Elizabeth added her own opinion.

"And Mary King is safe!"

It was evening before Elizabeth could be alone with Jane for the private chat she so longed for. She told Jane about Darcy's proposal and what he said in his letter about Wickham. She did not, however, tell Jane about what she had discovered as to why Bingley had not proposed to her. She knew her sister was quite broken-hearted and she did not wish to cause her any more pain. Elizabeth finished her account and asked her sister's opinion.

"Do you think I was wrong to refuse him?"

"Not at all."

"And what about Wickham?"

"Lizzy, I can hardly believe it! It's amazing how Wickham, who seems so nice and friendly, could be capable of such lies! Poor Mr Darcy!"

"But, Jane, do you think I should tell people the truth about Wickham's character?"

"I can see no reason to."

"I agree. Mr Darcy asked me not to talk about what happened to his sister, and if I try to discredit Wickham without this proof, no one will believe me. I have to respect his wishes. I would like Mr Wickham to be exposed for what he is but I am not the one to do it. He will be gone soon, anyway."

The days rolled slowly by until at last the regiment left Meryton for Brighton. Lydia was now far from unhappy, however, as she had been invited by Colonel Forster, the regiment's commander, to go to Brighton to stay with him and his wife for the summer. This meant she would be able to keep up her socialising with all the officers. This greatly alarmed Elizabeth, however, and she went to her father to try to persuade him not to let Lydia go.

"You know Lydia, she's very excitable and not at all sensible. In such a holiday atmosphere, she's sure to flirt. I fear she'll do something stupid, something that will be deeply embarrassing to her and to our family or even damage our reputation."

"Do not be uneasy, Lizzy. You and Jane are respected and so people forgive you for having three silly sisters. Colonel Forster will look after her, and she is too poor to attract someone who would take advantage of her. The officers will take more notice of wealthier young women."

Elizabeth had to be content with this.

At last, Mr and Mrs Gardiner arrived at Longbourn. Leaving their four young children to be looked after by Jane, they set off with Elizabeth. Stopping at several places on the way, such as Oxford, Warwick and Birmingham, it took them many days to reach Derbyshire. When they reached the county, they headed for the town of Lambton, where Mrs Gardiner had grown up. There they stayed at the inn. As luck would have it, Lambton was only five miles from Pemberley, Mr Darcy's estate, and Mrs Gardiner thought it would be a fine idea to pay a visit.

"I would love to see Pemberley again. It is truly a beautiful house and has some of the finest woods in the country."

For Elizabeth, the mere mention of anything to do with Mr Darcy brought to mind what had happened in Kent in the spring, and all her conflicting emotions associated with it. She could not refuse without telling her aunt of these events and she did not want to do that. So, after asking at the inn whether Mr Darcy was at home and discovering that he was not, she could think of no reason not to go to Pemberley.

Pemberley's grounds were, as Mrs Gardiner had promised, very beautiful. They were also huge. The three of them drove along the riverbank, through some woods and then up the hill towards the house. When they finally reached the house, Mrs Gardiner suggested they ask to be allowed to see inside. The housekeeper said she would show them round.

The house was huge, although they saw but a fraction of it. The rooms were full of elegant furniture and fine carpets. Elizabeth wondered what it would be like to live here rather than merely visit, and considered that had she accepted Darcy's proposal, she would have been mistress of it all.

Mr Gardiner spoke to the housekeeper.

"When do you expect Mr Darcy to return?"

"Tomorrow. He's coming with a large party of friends."

Elizabeth breathed a sigh of relief that they had not come a day later. Mrs Gardiner asked the housekeeper about a portrait.

"Is this Mr Darcy?"

"Yes, he's very handsome, don't you think?"

"He is indeed."

Mr Gardiner asked further.

"Does he live here for much of the year?"

"Maybe only about half of his time – not as much as I would wish."

Mr Gardiner continued.

"If he married, I'm sure he'd be here more often."

"Oh, yes, but I do not know when that might be. I don't know who's good enough for him."

Elizabeth couldn't help speaking up.

"It is a compliment to him that you think so."

"I'm only telling the truth, and what everybody who knows him would say. I've never had an angry word from him in my whole life, and I've known him since he was four."

This assessment of Mr Darcy's character was very surprising to Elizabeth. She had always thought of him as ill-tempered, but Mr Gardiner had to agree that few servants could speak so highly of their masters.

"You must feel very lucky."

"You're right there, sir. He was the sweetest, most generous boy when he was young, and he has remained so as a man."

Elizabeth could hardly believe the housekeeper's description of Darcy. Could she really be talking about the same man that Elizabeth knew? The woman continued on about her master.

"There's not one of the servants or tenants who would complain about him. Some people call him proud, but that's probably only because he doesn't say much."

As they moved on through the house, Elizabeth spotted a large portrait of Darcy. She stood before it for many minutes, studying the man's features. He was smiling in exactly the way she had seen him often in real life. How differently she now thought of him.

At last they finished the tour of the house, and were crossing the lawn in front of it. Then, about twenty yards in front of them, around a corner of the path, came Mr Darcy.

Disastrous News

On seeing Elizabeth and her companions, Mr Darcy started in surprise. Then he walked up to them. Elizabeth could feel herself blushing, and she looked away as he approached.

"It's a pleasure to see you again, Miss Bennet. Are you well?"

His voice sounded nervous. She turned to face him. He was smiling amiably.

"Yes, very well, thank you."

"Are you enjoying your visit to Pemberley?"

"Yes, it's a magnificent place."

Darcy continued asking her about her family and her trip to Derbyshire. He was somehow very different now. His manner had changed totally. Gone were the pride and the ill temper. She barely knew how to respond. After introducing himself to Mr and Mrs Gardiner, he offered to accompany them as they crossed the grounds back to their carriage.

As they went, Darcy and Mr Gardiner started to discuss fishing. Darcy said that there was excellent fishing in the river and invited Mr Gardiner to come and fish there. Darcy said he would even lend him equipment if he had none with him. As they talked, Elizabeth continued to be mystified by Darcy's changed manner.

What could have brought on this change, she wondered.

"It couldn't be me. After what I told him in Kent, I wouldn't have been surprised if he had snubbed me."

After a while, Elizabeth found herself walking next to Darcy, with Mr and Mrs Gardiner a little behind.

"We wouldn't have come had we known you would be here.

We were told you were away."

"I came back earlier than planned. The rest of my party are coming tomorrow. In fact, one of them, my sister Georgiana, particularly wants to meet you. May I introduce her to you during your stay at Lambton?"

"Yes, of course."

Elizabeth wondered why Georgiana Darcy might want to meet her, and realised that it could only be due to things that her brother had said. But after this there was an awkward silence. Elizabeth just did not know what to say.

When they reached the carriage, they said their goodbyes. On the ride back to the inn, Mr and Mrs Gardiner both expressed how Mr Darcy had exceeded their expectations. Elizabeth could still not explain it.

"I've been pleasantly surprised myself; I've never known him to be so polite before."

Mrs Gardiner, too, was puzzled.

"It's difficult to believe that someone so polite could have done what Mr Darcy did to Mr Wickham."

But Elizabeth was quick to defend him.

"Maybe we only know one side of that particular story."

The next day, Mr Darcy and Georgiana came to the inn in Lambton. Georgiana was a pretty girl of sixteen. She was very shy, and said very little. They did not stay long, but on leaving they invited Elizabeth and Mr and Mrs Gardiner to go to Pemberley for dinner. Many people would be there, including Mr Bingley and his sisters. Of course, they accepted the invitation.

That night, Elizabeth could not sleep. She could not keep thoughts of Mr Darcy out of her head. There were so many feelings.

She had stopped hating him long ago, and she deeply regretted ever having disliked him. Now he impressed her immensely with his kind, caring and polite manners and how he was so keen for her to meet his sister. She respected him for his popularity amongst his servants and tenants, and was grateful that he had forgiven her for the angry way she had rejected his proposal of marriage. She understood that he still had strong feelings for her and she wondered how deep her own feelings now went.

The next morning, Elizabeth received two letters from Jane. The first had taken a full five days to get to Lambton, whilst the second had been posted a day later. She had been about to leave for a walk with Mr and Mrs Gardiner, but she decided instead to stay in and read the letters. The first one went as follows:

"Dear Lizzy,

Something very serious and unexpected has happened. It concerns Lydia. Last night we received an express letter from Colonel Forster, saying that she has gone off to Scotland to get married to Mr Wickham. I am very sorry but willing to hope the best and hope that his intentions are good. He must know our father can give her nothing. Our mother is extremely upset, and everyone else, too. It's a good thing that we didn't tell anyone what we know about him. Lydia left a note for Mrs Forster to explain where they had gone. I must go, as mother needs me.

Jane"

Without pausing for breath, Elizabeth tore open the second letter.

"Dear Lizzy,

I have bad news. We have not found Lydia and Mr Wickham yet. Although we feel it would be foolish of Lydia to marry Mr Wickham, we are now anxious to learn it has taken place because there's good reason to think they have not gone to Scotland after all. Colonel Forster heard a rumour that Mr Wickham never intented to go to Scotland or to marry Lydia at all, so he left Brighton in an attempt to trace their route. He followed it easily to Clapham, but north of London there was no sign of their passing through. So they have probably remained in London. My dear Lizzy, I beg you all to come home soon. Father needs our uncle's advice and assistance. It's such a stressful time.

Jane"

Elizabeth rushed to the door in order to pursue Mr Gardiner and tell him of the situation. But just then the door opened, and a servant showed Mr Darcy in.

"I beg your pardon, Mr Darcy, but I must find Mr Gardiner at once on urgent business! I have not a moment to lose."

Darcy was clearly very concerned.

"Good heavens! What is the matter? Let the servant fetch Mr and Mrs Gardiner. You are not well."

This was done, and then Elizabeth felt suddenly weak, and put her hand out to the wall to support herself, as Darcy moved towards her.

"Can I get you anything? You are very ill."

Elizabeth sat down.

"No, thank you. There is nothing the matter with me. I am only upset because I've just had some dreadful news from Longbourn." She told him the news in Jane's letters and drew her own sad conclusion.

"Lydia is lost. She has no money, no connections, nothing that could ever tempt him. But I could have prevented it – if only I'd told everyone about the kind of person Wickham is!"

She buried her face in her handkerchief as she thought of the unhappy consequences of Lydia's foolishness.

"It's not just Lydia's life that will be ruined by this situation. If she's really living with Mr Wickham and not married, it will be a scandal that would not be forgotten. The reputation of the whole family would be affected by such deep shame."

Mr Darcy was truly understanding of Elizabeth's distress.

"I'm concerned for you, but I see that you would prefer to be alone right now. I suppose you won't be able to come to Pemberley today."

"No, we'll have to leave straight away. Please apologise for us and say urgent business calls us home at once. I beg you to conceal the unhappy truth for as long as possible."

As Darcy left, Elizabeth wondered whether she would ever see him again on such friendly terms as in recent days. She sighed when she looked back over their relationship and how her feelings had changed. She realised with regret that no one respectable would want to know her after they learned of Lydia's shameful behaviour. It was a real possibility that she would never see him again. An hour later, she was travelling with her aunt and uncle on the road to Longbourn.

Lydia's Way

When Elizabeth arrived home, it was to a home in great distress. There had been no further news of Lydia and Wickham, and Mr Bennet was still in London searching for them. Mrs Bennet was very busy blaming Colonel and Mrs Forster and accusing them of not keeping a proper eye on Lydia. She was also complaining that if all the family had gone to Brighton together, then none of this would have happened. Mr Gardiner said that he would go to London to help with the search, and this seemed to calm Mrs Bennet for the moment.

Elizabeth wanted to discover exactly what had happened. Jane told her that everyone had been caught off guard by the speed and closeness of Lydia and Wickham's attachment. Colonel Forster had known that Lydia liked Wickham's company, but he had had no idea to what extent. Then she showed Elizabeth the evidence.

"You haven't seen the note that Lydia left for Mrs Forster, have you? Here."

Elizabeth took the note, and read:

"Dear Harriet,

You will laugh when you know where I've gone, and I cannot help laughing myself at your surprise tomorrow morning, as soon as I'm missed. I'm going to Gretna Green to get married to Mr Wickham! I know this will all be a surprise for you, but I cannot be happy without him. You needn't let my family know – I'll write to them, too, when we're married, and sign my name Lydia Wickham.

*What a joke that will be! Give my love to Colonel Forster, and I
hope you will celebrate our good journey.*

Your affectionate friend,
Lydia Bennet"

As she read, Elizabeth grew increasingly horrified. Lydia did
not seem to understand the seriousness of what she was doing!
It all seemed little more than a joke to her, an entertaining game
in which no one could lose. Elizabeth was deeply worried.

"Lydia clearly thought they were going to get married."

Jane, too, was very concerned.

"Yes, but there's increasing doubt about this. Wickham has left
a great number of debts, including gambling debts, both in Meryton
and in Brighton, and Colonel Forster does not think he is honourable."

Mr Gardiner left immediately to help in the search for Lydia
and Wickham. Mrs Gardiner and the children returned home to
London a few days later and Mr Bennet returned to Longbourn
after having failed to locate the couple. Mr Bennet was philosophical
about the situation, although he was convinced that he was
primarily to blame.

Two days after Mr Bennet's return, he received an express letter
from Mr Gardiner. When the servant told Elizabeth, she rushed to
the library, breathless.

"What news, papa? Is it good or bad?"

Mr Bennet was joyless in his response.

"There's no good news to be expected in this affair. Here."

Gracechurch Street, London, Monday, August 2

"Dear Brother,

I have news at last about Lydia and Wickham, which I hope will be of relief to you. Soon after you left on Saturday, I managed to discover where they were living, and have since been able to speak to them both. They are not married, but if you can settle certain financial matters, I hope it will not be long before they are. You need to guarantee that they will receive Lydia's share of the inheritance plus an allowance of £100 per annum. It seems that Mr Wickham's circumstances are not as hopeless as they were believed to be and he is able to pay his debts and have enough money left to support Lydia. Send your answer as fast as you can and they will be married very shortly.

Edward Gardiner"

Elizabeth's worry turned to excitement.

"They are to be married? This is wonderful news. Have you answered the letter?"

"Not yet."

"It must be done right away! Consider how important every moment is in this situation."

Mr Bennet nervously agreed.

"Yes, Lizzy, but the terms worry me."

"But you must accept them."

"Yes, of course, but there are two things I'd like to know. How much money has your uncle put down to bring this about, and how am I ever going to pay him back?"

Elizabeth cried out in distress.

"Money? My uncle? Father, what do you mean?"

"Wickham would be a fool if he married Lydia for less than £10,000."

"£10,000? Oh, Father, how could you repay even half that amount?"

Mr Bennet said nothing and simply sat at his desk to write the letter.

With Lydia and Mr Wickham about to marry, Elizabeth began to allow her thoughts to stray back to what had happened in Derbyshire. She now regretted having told Mr Darcy about Lydia's elopement, caught as she was in a moment of great distress. Her regret did not come from a fear that Darcy would not keep it secret, but rather the effect it would have on him. Even without the scandal of Lydia and Wickham living together unmarried, she was sure that Darcy would not wish to associate with the Bennet family now that they were connected to a man he so rightly disliked.

She was embarrassed and ashamed. She felt sorry for herself and wanted to hear from him, although she felt there was now little chance of it. Now that she was convinced she could be happy with him, it was no longer likely they should meet.

If only he knew that the proposal she had rejected so strongly only four months ago would now be gladly accepted. In terms of personality, she believed that they matched each other perfectly. But she knew it was never to be.

A couple of days later, the Bennets received further news about Lydia and Mr Wickham. Wickham had been transferred, and after his marriage would serve in a regiment based in Newcastle, in the north of England. This was seen as a good opportunity to start his life anew.

Before they went, however, Lydia asked if they could come and stay at Longbourn for a week. At first, Mr Bennet refused, but after lengthy appeals from Jane and Elizabeth, he agreed.

On the day Lydia and Mr Wickham were due to arrive, the Bennet family were waiting in the breakfast room. They heard the carriage pull up in the drive outside. Mrs Bennet was smiling broadly, her husband was in deep and serious thought, and the daughters were anxious and uneasy.

Lydia's excited voice came from the hall, then the door was thrown open and she ran into the room. Mrs Bennet embraced her joyfully, and welcomed Mr Wickham warmly. The welcome from Mr Bennet and his daughters was less enthusiastic, but they all congratulated Lydia, and finally were able to sit down.

Mrs Bennet and Lydia seemed to have so much to say, and Elizabeth listened in silence. She was put off by Lydia's behaviour. Yes, she was married now, but she was still so wild and insensitive. But Lydia paid no mind to her sister's disapproval.

"You must all come to Newcastle over the winter. We can all go to the balls, and perhaps I'll be able to find a husband for one or two of my sisters."

Elizabeth was unmoved.

"Thank you, Lydia, but do not include me. I don't like your way of getting husbands."

Lydia completely ignored the comment, and instead asked after the neighbours, and announced how she longed to hear them calling her 'Mrs Wickham'.

One morning, not long after her arrival, Lydia was sitting with Elizabeth and Jane. Lydia was talking about her wedding day, giving an account of all the trivial details. Elizabeth was not really interested, and was barely listening, when her young sister mentioned that Mr Darcy had been there.

Elizabeth was shocked.

"Mr Darcy!"

"Yes, he had come with Wickham, you know. But oh, I quite forgot – I shouldn't have mentioned a word about Darcy. I promised faithfully not to mention him. What will Wickham say? It was a secret."

Jane cautioned Lydia to be careful.

"If it was supposed to be a secret, say no more about it."

Elizabeth agreed.

"Yes, we won't ask you any questions on the matter."

Elizabeth dropped the subject, though she was burning with curiosity.

That evening, Elizabeth wrote a letter to Mrs Gardiner to ask exactly why Mr Darcy had been at the wedding. Her reply came a couple of days later.

"Dear Niece,

Your uncle and I thought that you were fully aware of everything so we were surprised by your letter. If you are really unaware, then let me explain. On the day I arrived back in London, Mr Darcy called. He told us that he had found out where Wickham and Lydia were, and had seen and talked with them both.

He had tried to persuade Lydia to return to you, but she had refused. He had also discovered that Wickham had never intended to marry Lydia, but knew that Wickham would marry her if offered enough money. So Darcy had come to tell my husband that he would provide the necessary funds.

He did this because he thought he was to blame for not making public the nature of Wickham's character. He said if Wickham's worthlessness had been known, then no young woman of character would fall in love with him. He blamed his own pride for wanting to keep his affairs private. Mr Gardiner argued with Darcy for many hours about the money. But Mr Darcy stood firm, insisted on settling everything, and would not allow Mr Gardiner to contribute a penny.

Mr Darcy attended the wedding and made sure all matters were settled. However, it is still a secret and you must keep this to yourself. Tell only Jane, if you must.

Yours sincerely,
M Gardiner"

On reading this letter, Elizabeth was overcome by emotions. Her first reaction was to wonder why Mr Darcy had done all he had. Certainly Lydia had no idea that he was saving her reputation and her social standing, so Darcy could not have done it all for Lydia. Nor could it possibly be that Darcy had done it all for her. Why would he willingly associate with someone he so disliked for a woman who had already refused him? It didn't make sense. She decided that he must have swallowed his pride and corrected a situation he saw as partly his fault, and she admired him greatly for his honour and compassion.

Unexpected Endings

A few days later, Lydia and Mr Wickham left for Newcastle, and Longbourn became a quieter place. But some days after, there was news of a reappearance in the area – Mr Bingley was returning to Netherfield for the shooting season.

Elizabeth thought that Jane would be delighted by the news, but she was wrong.

"I saw you looking at me today, Lizzy, when we heard the news. But I know it's over – he won't have any interest in me. I so hope that we won't have to see too much of him."

But Elizabeth thought that Mr Bingley might have changed his mind about Jane, especially if Mr Darcy had told him about Jane's true feelings.

They were not too surprised that Mr Bingley came to visit Longbourn soon after he had arrived in Hertfordshire. Mrs Bennet saw him from a window as he was dismounting from his horse. But he was not alone, as Mrs Bennet excitedly remarked.

"It's Mr Darcy! Well, any friend of Mr Bingley's is always welcome here, even though I dislike the very sight of him."

Jane looked at Elizabeth, who was completely surprised that Mr Darcy should come.

Mrs Bennet welcomed Mr Bingley warmly, but she was considerably less friendly towards Mr Darcy. Elizabeth was hurt and distressed by this, as it was Mr Darcy who had saved Lydia's reputation, and her mother owed him a great debt of gratitude.

Most of the conversation took place between Mrs Bennet and Mr Bingley. Darcy looked very serious and hardly said a word, and Elizabeth was too embarrassed to even look at him. Before long, Bingley and Darcy left, although not without receiving an invitation to dine at Longbourn on Tuesday.

Elizabeth did not know what to make of it. Why, she wondered, did Darcy come at all, if all he is going to do is be silent and serious?

But Tuesday evening soon came. Mr Bingley, encouraged by Jane's smile, sat beside her at dinner, but Elizabeth found herself a long way from Mr Darcy. And whereas Jane and Bingley spoke to each other a lot, she was barely able to see Darcy. After dinner, matters were not much better. Elizabeth found herself sitting amongst a large group, and there were no free seats when Darcy came into the room. And later, when everyone sat down to play cards, Darcy was at a different table. The whole evening was incredibly frustrating for her.

The next day, Bingley came to Longbourn alone. Darcy had gone to London for ten days on business, but would return afterwards. Bingley stayed many hours that day, and returned the next. During the late afternoon, Elizabeth went into the breakfast room to write a letter. When she had finished, she returned to the drawing room.

On opening the door, she saw Jane and Bingley standing together by the fireplace, deeply engaged in conversation. As she entered, they turned quickly. Neither of them said anything, but the faces of both revealed that she had interrupted something important. Elizabeth thought about leaving, but Bingley, after whispering something in Jane's ear, rushed out of the room.

Jane came forward to embrace Elizabeth.

"I'm the happiest woman in the world! It's too much! I don't deserve it! Why isn't everyone else as happy as I?"

"He proposed?"

"And I accepted!"

"Wonderful!"

"Oh, Lizzy, I must go and tell Mother!"

One morning, about a week after Jane's engagement to Bingley, a very stylish carriage drove into Longbourn. The unexpected guest was shown into the drawing room, where Mrs Bennet and Elizabeth sat. It was Lady Catherine de Bourgh.

Lady Catherine stopped, and looked about her scornfully. Elizabeth welcomed her, but Lady Catherine gave barely a nod in return. After Elizabeth had introduced her mother, Lady Catherine voiced a few disapproving judgements about the house and gardens. Then she said:

"Miss Bennet, would you come for a walk with me in your gardens?"

It was more of an instruction than a request, but Elizabeth obeyed nonetheless. After they had been walking for about two minutes, Lady Catherine spoke again:

"Miss Bennet, you know why I am here."

"No, madam, not at all."

"Two days ago, I heard a rumour that you are to be engaged to my nephew, Mr Darcy. A rumour probably started by yourselves."

"I have never heard it."

"Well, let me tell you. This match cannot take place. Mr Darcy is engaged to my daughter. Now, what do you have to say?"

"Only this; that if he's already engaged to your daughter, then you can have no reason to suppose he will propose to me."

"Their engagement is of a peculiar kind. Ever since they were both young, it has been the wish of both his mother and me that they marry."

"It seems to me that Mr Darcy is a better judge of who he should marry than his mother and aunt."

"Stubborn, headstrong girl! You do not understand – my nephew and my daughter were formed for each other. They both come from wealthy, respectable and noble families. You, in contrast, do not have a suitable family background for him."

"If Mr Darcy does not object to my family background, then it should not concern you."

"Tell me once and for all, are you engaged to him?"

"I am not."

Lady Catherine seemed pleased.

"And will you promise me never to enter into such an engagement?"

"I shall not."

"Miss Bennet, I am shocked and amazed. I expected to find a more reasonable young woman. I think you should reconsider your reply."

"I'll never give you such a promise."

"You don't care, then, for the honour of my nephew!"

"Lady Catherine, I have nothing further to say. You know my answer."

"I am most seriously displeased."

And with that, Lady Catherine de Bourgh went straight to her carriage and drove away.

It was a few days after Lady Catherine's visit that Mr Bingley brought Darcy with him to Longbourn. They arrived early, and it was decided that the men, Jane, Elizabeth and Kitty would go for a walk. Bingley and Jane drifted away from the others, and Kitty only went as far as the Lucases'. In this way, Darcy and Elizabeth were soon walking alone together.

"Mr Darcy, I can't go on without thanking you for your extraordinary kindness to my poor sister. Ever since I have known, I have been anxious to tell you how grateful I am, and if my family knew of it, they would feel the same."

Mr Darcy looked surprised.

"I didn't want you to find out."

"Lydia betrayed the secret and then I could not rest until I knew everything. My family will always be in your debt."

"Well, if you want to thank me, do it for yourself alone because, although I respect your family, I did it only for you."

Elizabeth felt suddenly very embarrassed. After a short pause, Darcy went on.

"I must get something clear once and for all. If your feelings are still the same as they were last April, tell me now. My affections and wishes are unchanged, but one word from you will silence me on this subject forever."

After a short pause, Elizabeth told him that her feelings were quite the opposite of what they had been and she now felt the same as he did. Mr Darcy was very happy to hear this and they walked on, declaring to each other their deep feelings of love and respect. Darcy explained his optimism to Elizabeth.

"I began to feel hope when I saw Lady Catherine in London and she told me about the conversation she had had with you at Longbourn. I knew that if you had decided against me, you would have told her plainly and openly."

"Yes. You know me well enough to know that, after insulting you to your face, I would have no trouble insulting you to your relatives."

"My dearest Elizabeth, you have said nothing that I did not deserve. As a child I was given good principles but left to follow them in pride and self-importance. Without you I would still be doing so. You taught me a hard lesson, but I love you all the more for it."

They walked on, without knowing what direction they took. It was many hours before they returned to Longbourn, happy, tired and engaged.

The evening passed quietly, but Elizabeth was nervous because she anticipated what would be felt in the family when her engagement became known. She was aware that no one liked Mr Darcy but Jane. At night, she confided in her sister.

"You are joking, Lizzy. This cannot be – engaged to Mr Darcy!"

"Jane, this is a terrible beginning! I am sure nobody else will believe me, if you do not. I am telling the truth. He still loves me, and we are engaged."

"My dear, dear Lizzy, I congratulate you – but are you certain – are you quite certain that you can be happy with him?"

"There can be no doubt of that. We will be the happiest couple in the world."

"My dearest sister, how long have you loved him?"

"It has been coming on so gradually, that I hardly know when it began."

Elizabeth told her everything, including what happened at Pemberley and Lambton and his role in Lydia's marriage. Half the night was spent in conversation.

The next day Mr Bingley and Mr Darcy came to visit again, and after dinner Mr Darcy followed Mr Bennet into the library to ask for his consent to marry his daughter.

When he came back out a few minutes later, he smiled at Elizabeth and said that her father wished to speak to her now.

Her father was walking about the room, looking anxious.

"Lizzy, are you out of your senses, accepting this man? Haven't you always disliked him terribly?"

She explained the gradual change her feelings had undergone to her confused father.

"I love him. You do not know him as I do. He is not proud.

He is perfectly likeable, believe me."

"Well, my dear, I have no more to say. If this is the case, he deserves you. I could not have parted with you, my Lizzy, to anyone less worthy."

She then told him what Mr Darcy had done for Lydia. He listened with amazement.

Elizabeth's mind was now relieved from a very heavy weight, and she told her mother the news before she went to bed.

"Good gracious! Mr Darcy! Who would have thought it! Is it really true? Oh! My sweetest Lizzy! How rich you will be! I am so pleased. Such a charming man! So handsome! So tall! Oh, my dear Lizzy!"

Mrs Bennet was never so happy as on the day that her two eldest and most deserving daughters were married.

Activities

New Neighbours

Read or listen to Chapter 1 and write T (true) or F (false).

1 The new tenant in Netherfield Park is called
   Mr Bingley.   ....
2 Mrs Bennet thinks Mr Bingley would make a
   good husband for one of her daughters.   ....
3 Of all his daughters Mr Bennet favours Lydia the most. ....
4 Mr Bennet visits Mr Bingley without anyone in the
   family knowing.   ....
5 Mr Bingley does not seem very likeable at first.   ....
6 Elizabeth is offended by Mr Darcy's comments.   ....
7 Elizabeth thinks Mr Bingley's sisters are outgoing
   and have a good sense of humour.   ....
8 Despite his pride, Darcy is quite impressed by
   Elizabeth.   ....

What do you think?

A   Discuss the following questions.

1 Do Mr and Mrs Bennet receive the news of Mr Bingley's arrival
   in Longbourn in the same way? Comment on each one's
   reaction, referring to the text.
2 Mr Darcy leaves Elizabeth with a very bad impression. Do
   you think she is right to dislike him? Why (not)?
3 Do you think that someone's outward behaviour is always a
   reflection of what they are truly like? Or do you think
   appearances can be deceptive? Discuss.

Chapter 1

B   *Find the following extracts from Chapter 1 and discuss their meanings.*

1   p. 8: *'It is a truth universally acknowledged that a single man with a large fortune must be looking for a wife.'*

2   p. 9: *"Well, they're all silly and ignorant, of course, but Lizzy is a little quicker to understand things than her sisters."*

Language Practice

Fill in the gaps with the correct form of the words in capitals.

1	Mr Bennet has no .... to hearing his wife talk about the new tenant in Netherfield Park.	OBJECT
2	Mr Darcy thinks Elizabeth is .... but not pretty enough.	TOLERATE
3	Mr Bennet believes that all his daughters are silly and .... but Lizzy is a bit quicker to understand things.	IGNORE
4	Mr Bingley's sisters are much more .... dressed than any other woman at the ball in Meryton.	STYLE
5	Mrs Bennet and her five daughters reach the assembly rooms in Meryton early and eagerly await the .... of Mr Bingley and his party.	ARRIVE
6	Elizabeth thinks Mr Bingley's sisters are .... and self-important.	PRIDE
7	Mr Bingley has Mr Bennet's .... to marry whichever of his daughters he chooses.	PERMIT
8	Jane thinks .... of Mr Bingley's sisters, Mrs Hurst and Miss Bingley.	HIGH
9	Mrs Bennet cannot hide her excitement at Mr Bingley moving into the	NEIGHBOUR
10	Elizabeth watches Mr Bingley's party at the ball from a	DISTANT

Jane's Illness

 **Comprehension**

Read or listen to Chapter 2 and match the beginnings to the endings of the sentences below to make true statements.

1 ... When Elizabeth arrives at Netherfield to visit Jane,
2 ... Unlike his sisters, who are rather unconcerned about Jane,
3 ... Darcy agrees with Mrs Hurst and Miss Bingley
4 ... Mrs Bennet's visit to Netherfield
5 ... Elizabeth thinks it is very unlikely
6 ... When Miss Bingley fails to attract Darcy's attention,
7 ... Elizabeth jokingly suggests that she and Miss Bingley
8 ... Darcy's unforgiving nature

a that Darcy will take an interest in her.
b is a source of embarrassment for Elizabeth.
c is one of his many faults.
d Mr Bingley's sisters disapprove of the state she is in.
e punish Darcy for his shameful remarks.
f she takes Elizabeth for a walk around the room.
g Mr Bingley shows a genuine interest in her.
h that the Bennets' low social rank is an obstacle for them.

What do you think?

A Discuss the following questions.

1 Refer to the text to say what Mr Bingley's sisters are like. Does Elizabeth's impression of them at the Meryton ball prove to be right or wrong?
2 Judging from her behaviour in this chapter, what sort of person do you think Mrs Bennet is?
3 What do you think the differences are between living in the country and living in a town or city? Which do you prefer? Why?

B   *Find the following extracts from Chapter 2 and discuss their meanings.*

1   p. 20: 'This statement, having little to do with the truth, left Elizabeth blushing, and she quickly changed the subject.'

2   p. 23: "Yes, vanity is a fault. But pride is different. If the mind is superior, then pride can be hidden."

3   p. 23: 'Miss Bingley was now tired of a conversation from which she had been left out.'

Language Practice

Circle the correct word printed in bold.

1   Mr Darcy says that there is a greater **variety / vanity** of people in town than in the country.

2   Mrs Hurst has a high **remark / regard** for Jane and thinks she is a very sweet girl.

3   When Mrs Bennet finally leaves, it is a great **relief / response** to everyone at Netherfield.

4   Elizabeth thinks that Mr Bingley's house is in line with his **personality / presence**.

5   Mrs Hurst believes that the Bennets' lack of **status / state** makes it hard for Jane to find a good husband.

6   When Mrs Bennet exaggerates their social life, Elizabeth quickly changes the **matter / subject**.

7   For a long time Mrs Bennet continues to **entertain / embarrass** everyone with the stupidity of her remarks.

8   Elizabeth notices that Miss Bingley and Mrs Hurst are rather **uncomfortable / unconcerned** about Jane when she isn't present.

9   When Elizabeth is invited to stay at Netherfield until her sister gets better, she **gratefully / naturally** accepts the offer.

10   Mr Darcy doesn't join Elizabeth and Miss Bingley for a walk around the room, as he doesn't want to **interfere / intrude** on their privacy.

93

Mr Collins and Mr Wickham

 **Comprehension**

Read or listen to Chapter 3 and fill in the names.

1 .... is looking for a wife.
2 .... tells Mr Collins that Jane will soon be engaged.
3 .... holds a dinner party at her home.
4 .... and Lydia are very excited about meeting officers.
5 .... asks Elizabeth questions about Mr Darcy.
6 .... holds a ball at Netherfield.
7 .... is concerned about Elizabeth's respect for Mr Wickham.
8 .... tells Elizabeth that Mr Wickham has been telling her stories.
9 .... tells Elizabeth that Mr Bingley does not know Mr Wickham personally.
10 .... believes that Darcy has wronged Wickham.

What do you think?

A Discuss the following questions.

1 Judging from the text, what is your opinion of Mr Collins?
2 How do Mr Wickham's words affect Elizabeth's feelings about Darcy? Are Mr and Miss Bingley also affected? Why (not)?
3 Do you think it is proper to discuss personal issues, especially if they concern someone else?

B Find the following extracts from Chapter 3 and discuss their meanings.

1 p. 27: *"Maybe he couldn't bear the thought of my having something granted by his father."*
2 p. 27: *"Mr Wickham has indeed got a pleasant manner that ensures he makes many friends, but he has a problem keeping them."*

Language Practice

I *Use the verbs in the box to fill in the blanks and make collocations. Then fill in the sentences below, putting the verbs in the correct form.*

> • bear • catch • attend • make(x2)
> • set up • have • join

1	.... the thought	5	.... camp
2	.... no doubt	6	.... a ball
3	.... sb off guard	7	.... the army
4	.... amends	8	.... sense

1 Wickham won't be .... the ball at Netherfield because he has to go to London on business.

2 Although Mr Bingley hasn't heard the whole story, he .... no doubt that Darcy hasn't wronged Wickham.

3 Lydia and Kitty can't wait to meet the officers who have .... camp near Meryton.

4 Wickham thinks that Darcy couldn't .... the thought of him having something granted by the late Mr Darcy.

5 Mr Collins sees his marriage to one of the Bennet girls as a way for him to .... amends for inheriting their father's estate.

6 Wickham is left with no choice but to .... the army, when Darcy prevents him from becoming a priest.

7 Darcy .... Elizabeth off guard when he suddenly comes up to her and asks her to dance with him.

8 After talking to Jane, it all .... sense to Elizabeth, who is convinced of Darcy's shameful behaviour to Wickham.

II *Look at the word list for Chapter 3. Use ten words/phrases from it to write a summary of the chapter.*

A Wedding

📖 Comprehension 🎧

Read or listen to Chapter 4 and correct the mistakes.

1   Mr Collins assumes Kitty would be happy to marry him.
2   Mr Bennet is very upset that Elizabeth has refused Mr Collins' proposal.
3   Elizabeth hurts Mr Collins' feelings with her rejection.
4   Jane is very disappointed that Elizabeth won't see Darcy for the whole winter.
5   Charlotte tries to direct Mr Collins' attentions back onto Elizabeth.
6   To Elizabeth's delight, Charlotte accepts Mr Collins' marriage proposal.
7   Mrs Gardiner advises Elizabeth to encourage Wickham.
8   Elizabeth cannot compete with Miss King's beauty.

What do you think?

A   Discuss the following questions.

1   Elizabeth and Charlotte appear to be very different from each other as characters. Refer to the text to explain how.
2   What can you tell about Mr and Mrs Bennet's relationship? Who do you think the head of the family is? Why?
3   What do you think Elizabeth's stay in Kent will be like? Explain.

B   Find the following extracts from Chapter 4 and discuss their meanings.

1   p. 31: *"Come now, I know it's the custom for you young ladies to refuse the first offer, but just think about what it is you're turning down."*

2   p. 33: *"This leaves you with an unfortunate choice. Your mother will never see you again if you do not marry Mr Collins, and I will never see you again if you do."*

Language Practice

I Fill in the gaps with the correct prepositions.

1 Elizabeth does not think ill .... either Mr Wickham or Miss King.

2 After considering Mrs Gardiner's point .... view, Elizabeth takes her advice about Mr Wickham.

3 Elizabeth is certain that Wickham has no interest .... marrying her.

4 There is more .... stake for Charlotte than merely keeping Mr Collins happy.

5 Elizabeth's surprise at Charlotte's engagement is nothing compared .... her amazement that she is marrying purely for money.

6 Charlotte's parents joyfully give their consent .... her marriage with Mr Collins.

7 Elizabeth confides .... her aunt all her hopes and concerns about Jane and Mr Bingley.

8 Unlike Mr Bennet, who doesn't want Elizabeth to accept Mr Collins' proposal, Mrs Bennet is .... herself that her daughter rejects such an opportunity.

II Match the words to the definitions.

1 bitterly   a to make sb believe that sth is the right thing to do

2 suspect

3 unlikely   b to get closer

                c to make sb believe sth that is not true; cheat

4 distant

5 disastrous   d cold and unfriendly

6 approach   e in a way that shows anger

                f extremely bad; terrible

7 deceive   g improbable to happen

8 persuade   h to believe sth is probably true

A Month in Kent

 Comprehension

Read or listen to Chapter 5 and circle the correct answers.

1   Elizabeth thinks her evening at Rosings is ...
   a   a privilege.
   b   a bit disturbing.
   c   an opportunity for her to see Lady Catherine's grand and elegant home.

2   Elizabeth doubts that Darcy will want Anne as his wife because ...
   a   this is only Lady Catherine's wish.
   b   his sister's company is enough for him.
   c   Anne looks like a very weak and ill child.

3   What Darcy thinks of Elizabeth is that ...
   a   she is very courageous.
   b   she is right about him trying to bully her.
   c   her opinion of him is influenced by other people.

4   Regarding Darcy's reluctance to meet new people, Elizabeth ...
   a   thinks he should make a greater effort.
   b   realises she also lacks the skill to play the piano better.
   c   understands his difficulty in talking with people he hasn't met before.

5   Darcy's sister proves to be ...
   a   badly-behaved.
   b   difficult to manage.
   c   his only company.

6   Bingley changes his mind about proposing to Jane because ...
   a   Darcy advises him against doing so.
   b   she lacks wealth and connections.
   c   he is attracted to Darcy's sister.

What do you think?

A **Discuss the following questions.**

1 Do you think Elizabeth shares Mr Collins' opinion about Lady Catherine's 'fine qualities', especially after her visit to Rosings?

2 What personal experience does Elizabeth refer to in order to prove to Darcy that he is responsible for his poor social skills? Do you agree with her? Why (not)?

3 Like Wickham earlier, Colonel Fitzwilliam affects Elizabeth's opinion of Darcy immensely. Explain.

B **Find the following extracts from Chapter 5 and discuss their meanings.**

1 p. 40: "*About music! Then let's hear it. There are few people in England, I suppose, who have more true enjoyment of music than I, or a better natural taste. If I'd ever learnt, I would have been an expert pianist.*"

2 p. 44: "*I'm surprised he doesn't marry, because then he would have constant companionship.*"

Language Practice

Fill in the gaps with the words in the box.

• reluctant • privilege • ability • agreeably • stubborn • mistaken

1 Elizabeth does not lack the .... to play the piano better; all she needs is more practice.

2 Colonel Fitzwilliam responds .... to Lady Catherine's comment about music.

3 Elizabeth is .... to reveal her age to Lady Catherine.

4 Elizabeth would be .... to think that Darcy is trying to bully her.

5 Mr Collins thinks it's a .... to be invited to Rosings.

6 Elizabeth can be very .... when bullied.

Darcy Opens his Heart

 Comprehension

Read or listen to Chapter 6 and circle the answer that is not correct.

1 After talking to Colonel Fitzwilliam, Elizabeth ...
   a does not feel comfortable seeing Darcy at Rosings.
   b expects him to visit her and ask after her health.

2 When Darcy comes to the parsonage, Elizabeth ...
   a finds him to be very nervous.
   b struggles against her feelings for him.

3 When Darcy proposes to Elizabeth, she ...
   a finds it difficult to accept because of her low social standing.
   b is completely surprised and offended by the offer.

4 Ever since Elizabeth met Darcy, she ...
   a has thought he is very conceited.
   b has been thinking of the possibility of marrying him.

5 Darcy's letter to Elizabeth ...
   a praises the behaviour of Elizabeth's family.
   b makes her think that he might have been telling the truth about Mr Wickham.

6 Elizabeth begins to realise that Wickham ...
   a is someone she can trust with personal information.
   b talked to her about the sorts of personal things a gentleman would not tell a stranger.

7 When Elizabeth returns to the parsonage after reading Darcy's letter, she ...
   a no longer thinks that Darcy is inconsiderate to the feelings of others.
   b feels sorry to have missed Darcy and Fitzwilliam.

What do you think?

A Discuss the following questions.

1 What are Elizabeth's reasons for turning Darcy's proposal down? Do you think she is right to feel this way? Why (not)?

2 How does Darcy's letter change Elizabeth's opinion about him? Do you think she has been mistaken about him so far?

3 Is it a good idea for Darcy to explain everything to Elizabeth in a letter? Do you think the outcome would still be the same if he attempted to talk to her instead? Justify your answer.

B Find the following extracts from Chapter 6 and discuss their meanings.

1 p. 47: 'Darcy sat down, said nothing, then after half a minute stood again, and walked around the room. Elizabeth did not know what to say.'

2 p. 48: 'She knew of course that she would never accept his proposal, but for a moment she felt sorry for him, since she knew the pain of rejection would be great.'

Language Practice

Complete the sentences using the following phrasal verbs in the correct form.

• hold back • back up • use up • catch up with • take up

1 Darcy assures Elizabeth that Fitzwilliam can .... everything he has written in his letter.

2 After Elizabeth's refusal to marry Darcy, he leaves immediately so as not to .... any more of her time.

3 Mr Wickham .... all of Darcy's money on high living.

4 Jane gave Darcy the impression that she was .... something ....

5 When Elizabeth hears Darcy calling her name, she starts walking away but he .... her.

Pemberley

 **Comprehension**

Read or listen to Chapter 7 and complete the sentences, using one word.

1 The news of the regiment leaving Meryton is the worst news .... for Lydia.

2 During their private ...., Elizabeth tells Jane about Darcy's proposal.

3 Although Elizabeth wants Mr Wickham to be ...., she has to respect Darcy's wishes regarding his sister.

4 Elizabeth worries that Lydia will embarrass herself and her family, as she is very excitable and not .... at all.

5 The incident in Kent caused Elizabeth .... emotions.

6 The visitors to Pemberley only see a .... of the house, which is huge.

7 When Mrs Gardiner asks the .... at Pemberley about Darcy's portrait, they engage in conversation about him.

8 Elizabeth is surprised to hear such compliments about Darcy, who has always appeared to be .... to her.

What do you think?

A Discuss the following questions.

1 Do you think Elizabeth is right not to tell Jane about Darcy advising Bingley not to marry her? Why (not)?

2 Refer to the text to describe Lydia as a character. How similar to/different from Elizabeth is she?

3 Following Darcy's letter, Elizabeth's visit to Pemberley also affects her greatly as to her opinion of Darcy. Explain.

4 Considering their last encounter in Kent, how do you think Elizabeth and Darcy feel to run into each other at Pemberley?

B *Find the following extracts from Chapter 7 and discuss their meanings.*

1 p. 58: *'Elizabeth breathed a sigh of relief that they had not come a day later.'*

2 p. 60: *"Some people call him proud, but that's probably only because he doesn't say much."*

Language Practice

Use the correct forms of the phrases in the box to complete the sentences.

> • take advantage of • breathe a sigh of relief • pay a visit
> • bring (sth) to mind • take notice of • speak highly of

1 Mr Bennet thinks the officers in Brighton will .... wealthier young women and not be attracted by Lydia.

2 Few servants can .... as .... their masters as the housekeeper at Pemberley.

3 Since they are so close to Darcy's estate, the Gardiners and Elizabeth think it's a fine idea to ....

4 For Elizabeth, the mere mention of Darcy's name .... the incident in Kent.

5 None of the officers is likely to .... Lydia, as she is too poor.

6 Elizabeth .... that she and the Gardiners have come to Pemberley before Darcy.

What happens next?

Think about the following ideas and guess which one happens next in the story.

Darcy gets very upset to find Elizabeth and the Gardiners at Pemberley.	Elizabeth accepts Darcy's marriage proposal.
	Lydia's foolish behaviour puts her family in a difficult situation.

Chapter 8

Disastrous News

📖 Comprehension 🎧

Read or listen to Chapter 8 and fill in the gaps in the following text, using a word or phrase.

Darcy is very surprised to see Elizabeth at Pemberley. However, he is smiling 1) .... and shows great interest in her trip to Derbyshire. His pride and 2) .... are gone and he is very polite. He even offers to lend Mr Gardiner 3) .... if he wishes to go fishing in the river. He is particularly friendly to Elizabeth and wants to introduce her to his sister, Georgiana. The Gardiners can't help commenting that Darcy has exceeded their 4) ....
As for Elizabeth herself, she is as pleasantly surprised.
The next day, Darcy and Georgiana invite the three of them to Pemberley for dinner. Elizabeth is 5) .... by Darcy's manners and realises he still has strong feelings for her. The next morning, however, holds an even bigger surprise for Elizabeth. She finds out that Lydia has gone off to Scotland to marry Mr Wickham. Colonel Forster has set out in an attempt to 6) .... their route but with no success. Elizabeth is very upset at Lydia's 7) .... She asks Darcy to apologise for her and her aunt and uncle at Pemberley and say 8) .... business calls them back home. At the same time, she can't help worrying that she might not see Darcy again.

What do you think?

A Discuss the following questions.

1 Darcy's character in this chapter sharply contrasts with the one we've been presented with so far. Discuss.

2 Comment on the impact Lydia's foolish behaviour is likely to have on all the members of her family. Do you think they are right to worry so much?

3 Judging from this chapter, how united do you think the members of the Bennet family are? Explain.

B   *Find the following extracts from Chapter 8 and discuss their meanings.*

1   p. 61: "It couldn't be me. After what I told him in Kent, I wouldn't have been surprised if he had snubbed me."
2   p. 63: "Maybe we only know one side of that particular story."
3   p. 65: "I beg your pardon, Mr Darcy, but I must find Mr Gardiner at once on urgent business! I have not a moment to lose."

Language Practice

Imagine Elizabeth didn't talk to Darcy in person about her family's predicament but wrote a letter instead. Read Chapter 8 again and write Elizabeth's letter to Darcy, explaining the situation and expressing her regret that she won't be able to attend dinner at Pemberley.

Date

Dear Mr Darcy,

Introduction – State the subject of your letter.

Main body – Develop the points you have made in the introduction.

Conclusion – Summarise what you have said and express your feelings about the situation.

Elizabeth Bennet

Lydia's Way

Comprehension

Read or listen to Chapter 9 and put the events in the correct chronological order.

a   ....   The prospect of Lydia and Wickham's marriage makes Elizabeth sad about her future with Darcy.

b   ....   Jane shows Elizabeth Lydia's note to Mrs Forster.

c   ....   Lydia reveals that Darcy was at her wedding.

d   ....   Mr Gardiner goes to London to search for Lydia and Wickham.

e   ....   Mr Bennet receives some reassuring news about Lydia and Wickham.

f   ....   Elizabeth writes to Mrs Gardiner, who informs her niece about Darcy's involvement in the wedding.

g   ....   Lydia and Wickham come to Longbourn for a visit.

What do you think?

A   Discuss the following questions.

1   How is Lydia's attitude contrasted to everyone else's in the family? Does her marriage make her more mature?

2   What are the reasons that make Elizabeth regret telling Darcy about Lydia's elopement? Do you think she is right to worry?

3   According to Mrs Gardiner's letter, what are the reasons that lead Darcy to intervene in Lydia's wedding? Do you think these are the only reasons for him to act the way he does?

B   Find the following extracts from Chapter 9 and discuss their meanings.

1   p. 68: 'Mrs Bennet was very busy blaming Colonel and Mrs Forster and accusing them of not keeping a proper eye on Lydia.'

2   p. 73: 'This was seen as a good opportunity to start his life anew.'

Language Practice

Fill in the crossword, using vocabulary from Chapter 9.

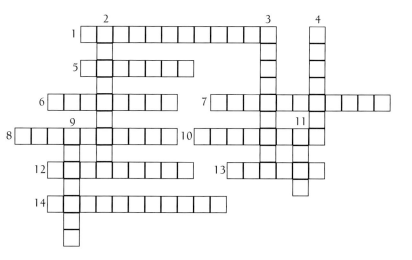

Across

1 showing your love for sb
5 not knowing or realising sth
6 to move from one place to another
7 not noticing other people's feelings
8 to give money
10 sth that proves sth else is true
12 in a way that shows you want to do sth
13 to pay an amount of money
14 the act of showing that sb's behaviour or ideas are not acceptable

Down

2 relating to money
3 the act of going away secretly with sb in order to get married
4 to give, to make available
9 unimportant
11 to make sb feel less angry or worried

Unexpected Endings

 **Comprehension**

Read or listen to Chapter 10 and answer the following questions.

1 Why is Mr Bingley returning to Netherfield?
2 Who is Mr Bingley visiting Longbourn with?
3 How does dinner at Longbourn turn out for Elizabeth?
4 How does Bingley make Jane extremely happy?
5 What is the purpose of Lady Catherine's visit to Longbourn?
6 What does Darcy say about his feelings for Elizabeth when he visits her at Longbourn?
7 Why were Darcy's good principles useless until he met Elizabeth?
8 Why does Darcy follow Mr Bennet into the library after dinner?

What do you think?

A Discuss the following questions.

1 When Jane first hears that Mr Bingley is returning to Longbourn, she doesn't wish to see much of him. Soon, however, her attitude changes and she even ends up engaged to him. Comment on the gradual change of their relationship.

2 What do you think of Elizabeth's attitude to Lady Catherine? What does it tell about her character? Do you remember any other incidents in the story where again Elizabeth's attitude was not the one conventionally expected?

3 What lesson does Elizabeth teach Darcy? How does she manage to bring out the best in him?

B Find the following extracts from Chapter 10 and discuss their meanings.

1 p. 79: *"It's Mr Darcy! Well, any friend of Mr Bingley's is always welcome here, even though I dislike the very sight of him."*

2 p. 84: *"Well, if you want to thank me, do it for yourself alone because, although I respect your family, I did it only for you."*

What's the moral?

The moral in a story is a lesson about what is right or wrong. What do you think the moral is in 'Pride & Prejudice'? Choose one or more of the following statements or create your own moral of the story. Explain your answer in either case.

1 Pride can be destructive.
2 To see the world clearly, you must be free of pride and prejudice.
3 You should never judge people on first impressions.
4 It is better to marry for love than for money.
5 Most people never change.
6 Love makes the world go round.
7 Your own moral: ....

Culture Corner

In *Pride and Prejudice*, Mr Wickham and Lydia set out for Gretna Green, a small village in the south of Scotland, near the border with England. Gretna Green is very famous for being the place where tens of thousands of runaway marriages have been performed. This began in 1753, when an act of parliament was passed in England requiring parental consent to the marriage if a partner was under age 21. This did not apply in Scotland, however, where boys could be married at 14 and girls at 12, regardless of parental consent. Since Gretna Green was the first village across the border in Scotland, that is where elopers got married.

In Gretna Green, most of the ceremonies were performed by local blacksmiths, who became known as 'anvil priests'. Today, thousands of couples are still married 'over the anvil', and Gretna Green remains one of the most popular wedding venues in the world.

Choose a village or a small town from your own or another country that is famous for some interesting tradition or product. Research its history and popularity and present your findings to the class. Use drawings, pictures and photographs to enhance your presentation.

Weddings

Marriage is a prevalent theme in "Pride and Prejudice", being Mrs Bennet's constant concern as regards her daughters. In Jane Austen's time, education and professions were not accessible to women, whose only chance of having an income was either by getting married or receiving an inheritance. Marriage, therefore, was always seen in connection with money and respectability, and was the only way for a young woman to secure herself financially and not become an old maid.

No matter how different woman's position is today, all human societies embrace the institution of marriage. Every culture has its own distinctive way of celebrating a wedding, placing emphasis on every single aspect of it, including clothing, food, music and rituals. These all have symbolic meaning. Examples include the following:

Clothing

In China, the bride and groom both usually wear red, since red Is traditionally the colour of happiness and good fortune. The phoenix symbol is woven into the bride's clothing whereas the groom's clothes bear a woven pattern of the dragon symbol. These symbols are rooted in ancient Chinese mythology.

Food

The traditional French wedding cake, called croquembouche, or crunch in the mouth, consists of buns filled with crème patisserie, built into a pyramid and decorated with fine strands of caramel. Other Western wedding cakes are made in tiers and have miniature figurines of the bride and groom on the top.

Music

In Romania, the Lautari are traditional musicians who perform traditional Gypsy songs at weddings. Since the ceremonies can last 48 hours, they also provide other entertainment, such as magic tricks and storytelling, and generally guide the participants through the rituals.

Rituals

Handfasting is a Celtic wedding ritual in which couples in Scotland or England clasp each other's hands, and then all four hands are tied together with a cord or ribbon. Handfasting is the origin of the common expression "tying the knot".

Jumping the broom was first known in Wales but it was originally a West African custom. Today it is a common way to end a wedding in some African-American communities. By jumping the broom, the bride and groom symbolically sweep away their single lives and leap into their shared life as a married couple.

Choose a country or culture – either your own or another – and research how the wedding ceremonies are performed there. Describe and discuss the different aspects of the ceremony to the class, such as the clothes, the food, the music and the rituals, explaining what they symbolise. Use the examples above as guidelines for your presentation. Use photographs, drawings, quotations and other descriptive items to make your presentation as interesting as possible.

111

Letters

Notes and letters were the predominant form of communication in Jane Austen's time, making the whole process of writing into an art. Letter writing could indeed be a laborious task requiring a proper set of materials, including a quill pen, an inkstand and sometimes a writing box; a small box for storing writing materials and carrying them around. After writing the letter, the sender folded the paper and sealed it with a wax seal. Apart from laborious, letter writing could be expensive as well, depending on the size of the letter and the distance it travelled. However, no one can deny the beauty of letter writing, even today that communication is much easier and more affordable.

1 *In "Pride & Prejudice" many notes and letters are sent and received. Imagine that the following excerpts are parts of the characters' correspondence in Chapters 2, 3 and 4. Read them carefully and decide which note or letter writing occasion each one corresponds to.*

A

Dear Miss Bennet,
As urgent business calls my brother back to London, we are all leaving Netherfield for the winter.

B

Don't have the slightest doubt that our Jane is in good hands. I'm sure my presence here will be of benefit to her as well.

Elizabeth

C
Again, I apologise for any discomfort or inconvenience I might have caused and look forward to finding a way to compensate for it.
Yours Sincerely,
William Collins

D
Dear Miss Bennet,
My sister and I would be delighted to have your company at dinner tonight.

E
Dear Mr Bennet,
We do not wish to alarm you and your family with this letter but we must inform you that Miss Bennet has fallen ill, probably due to the weather. We, therefore, think it wise to keep her in our care until she recovers.

11 *Imagine you are the recipient of one of the notes and letters above. Respond to it with a note or letter of your own.*

Word List

Look up these words/phrases in the dictionary and write their meanings.

Chapter 1

acknowledge (v) ....

affect (v) ....

announce (v) ....

arrival (n) ....

assembly rooms (pl n) ....

attract attention (phr) ....

await (v) ....

ball (n) ....

be in good spirits (was – been) (phr) ....

be taken by sth (was – been)(phr) ....

break the news (broke – broken) (phr) ....

character (n) ....

close by (phr) ....

come of (sth) (came – come) (phr v) ....

company (n) ....

compliment (n) ....

concern (n) ....

deserve (v) ....

differ (v) ....

eagerly (adv) ....

eldest (adj) ....

favour (v) ....

figure (n) ....

fortune (n) ....

from a distance (phr) ....

good looks (n) ....

handsome (adj) ....

ignorant (adj) ....

ignore (v) ....

introduce (v) ....
let (let – let) (v) ....
local (adj) ....
make out (made – made) (phr v) ....
move in (phr v) ....
necessary (adj)..
neighbour (n) ....
neighbourhood (n) ....
nerves (pl n) ....
newcomer (n) ....
notice (v) ....
objection (n) ....
opportunity (n) ....
outgoing (adj)...
overhear (overheard – overheard) (v) ....
party (n) ....
permission (n) ....
play along (phr v) ....
pound (v) ....
praise (v) ....
pride (n) ....
promise (v) ....
proud (adj) ....
public (adj) ....
receive (v) ....
repair (v) ....
reply (n) ....
respond (v)..
rude (adj) ....
rumour (n) ....
seated (adj)
self-important (adj) ....
sense of humour (phr) ....
single (adj) ....

slightly (adv) ....
spread (spread – spread) (v) ....
stylishly (adv)..
tease (v) ....
tempt (v) ....
think highly/well of sb (thought – thought) (phr) ....
tolerable (adj) ....
universally (adv) ....
wealth (n) ....
wealthy (adj) ....
well thought of (phr) ....
well-dressed (adj) ....
well-educated (adj) ....
well-mannered (adj)...

Chapter 2

accept an offer (phr) ....
advantage (n) ....
amused (adj) ....
annoyed (adj) ....
ask after (phr v) ....
assure (v) ....
bedside (n) ....
blush (v) ....
care for (phr v) ....
carriage (n) ....
chance (n) ....
change the subject (phr) ....
character (n) ....
concerned (adj) ....
condition (n) ....
conversation (n) ....
convinced (adj) ....
cooly (adv) ....

criticise (v) ....

dare (v) ....

defend (v) ....

disagree (v) ....

disappointed (adj) ....

disapprove (v) ....

displeased (adj) ....

embarrass (v)..

entertain (v) ....

especially (adv)..

fault (n) ....

fever (n) ....

flatter (v) ....

genuine (adj) ....

gratefully (adv) ....

have a high regard for sb (had – had) (phr) ....

human nature (n)..

in line with (phr) ....

increase (v) ....

inform (v) ....

insist (v) ....

interfere (in) (v) ....

intrude (on) (v) ....

invitation (n)...

keep sb company (kept – kept) (phr) ....

lack (n) ....

lively (adj) ....

look down on sb (phr v).......................................

major (adj) ....

make fun of (made – made) (phr) ....

matter (n) ....

messy (adj) ....

mistaken (adj)..

misunderstand (misunderstood – misunderstood) (v) ....

117

mud (n) ....
muddy (adj) ....
naturally (adv) ....
nearness (n) ....
observe (v) ....
on horseback (phr) ....
overnight (adv) ....
personality (n) ....
pick on (phr v) ....
please (v) ....
pleased (adj) ....
presence (n) ....
pretend (v) ....
privacy (n) ....
private (adj) ....
punish (v) ....
refuse (v) ....
relief (n) ....
remain (v) ....
remark (n/v) ....
reply (n) ....
response (n) ....
send for (sent – sent) (phr v) ....
sense (v) ....
set off (set – set) (phr v) ....
shameful (adj) ....
shift (v) ....
show off (showed – shown) (phr v)....................
state (n) ....
statement (n) ....
status (n) ....
stay overnight (phr) ....
stupidity (n) ....
subject (n) ....

superior (adj) ....

tempt (v) ....

uncomfortable (adj) ....

unconcerned (adj) ....

unforgiving (adj) ....

value (n) ....

vanity (n) ....

variety (n) ....

victory (n) ....

view (n) ....

weakness (n) ....

wilfully (adv) ....

Chapter 3

absence (n) ....

apologise (for) (v) ....

apology (n) ....

army (n) ....

associate with (v) ....

attend (v) ....

bear (v) ....

card table (n) ....

catch sb off guard (caught – caught) (phr) ....

charming (adj) ....

choice (n) ....

clumsy (adj) ....

confirm (v) ....

costly (adj) ....

critical (adj) ....

cruelly (adv) ....

declare (v) ....

disappointment (n) ....

discomfort (n) ....

disgrace (v) ....

doubt (n) ....

encourage (v) ....

engaged (adj) ....

ensure (v) ....

estate (n) ....

expect (v) ....

expectation (n) ....

expression (n) ....

fulfil (v) ....

further (adv) ....

get on with (got – got) (phr v) ....

grant (v) ....

heartily (adv) ....

honest (adj) ....

horrified (adj) ....

inherit (v) ....

inheritance (n) ....

inquire (v) ....

insult (n) ....

intended (adj) ....

intention (n) ....

jealousy (n) ....

join (v) ....

length (n) ....

look forward to (phr v) ....

magnificence (n) ....

magnificent (adj) ....

make amends (made – made) (phr) ....

make sense (made – made) (phr) ....

mention (v) ....

notable (adj) ....

noticeable (adj) ....

noticeably (adv) ....

notion (n) ....

officer (n) ....

patroness (n) ....

post (n) ....

prevent (v) ....

priest (n) ....

publicly (adv) ....

pursue (v) ....

radiant (adj) ....

realise (v) ....

regiment (n) ....

request (v) ....

respect (n) ....

set up camp (set – set) (phr) ....

shocking (adj) ....

situation (n) ....

switch (v) ....

take up (took – taken) (phr v) ....

term (n) ....

train (v) ....

truthful (adj) ....

turn out (phr v) ....

uniform (n) ....

unintended (adj) ....

version (n) ....

wrong (v) ....

Chapter 4

amazement (n) ....

approach (v) ....

at stake (phr) ....

attractive (adj) ....

be beside oneself (was – been) (phr) ....

bitterly (adv) ....

boldly (adv) ....

broken-hearted (adj) ....

can't help doing sth (phr) ....

carefree (adj) ....

carry on (phr v) ....

certainty (n) ....

change one's mind (phr) ....

come to the point (came – come) (phr) ....

comfort (v) ....

compare (v) ....

compete (v) ....

complain (v) ....

confide (in) (v) ....

consent (n) ....

convince (v) ....

custom (n) ....

dawn (n) ....

deceive (v) ....

demand (v) ....

disastrous (adj) ....

disbelief (n) ....

distant (adj) ....

doubt (v) ....

dowry (n) ....

draw attention away from (drew – drawn) (phr) ....

drop (v) ....

engage (in) (v) ....

engagement (n) ....

enormous (adj) ....

establish (v) ....

explanation (n) ....

get over (got – got) (phr v) ....

grateful (adj) ....

handle (v) ....

hasty (adj) ....

have a word with sb (had – had)(phr) ....

have no interest in sth (had – had) (phr) ....

intercept (v) ....

joyfully (adv) ....

lane (n) ....

lengthy (adj) ....

make a move (made – made) (phr) ....

merely (adv) ....

nod (v) ....

occupy (v) ....

one's side of the matter (phr) ....

peaceful (adj) ....

persuade (v) ....

point of view (n) ....

profession (n) ....

proposal (n) ....

propose (v) ....

purely (adv) ....

redirect (v) ....

regularly (adv) ....

rejection (n) ....

relationship (n) ....

romantic (n) ....

rope (v) ....

rush (v) ....

scheme (n) ....

sneak (v) ....

success (n) ....

summon (v) ....

suspect (v) ....

swiftly (adv) ....

take sb's advice (took – taken) (phr) ....

think ill of sb (thought – thought) (phr) ....

turn down (phr v) ....

unfortunate (adj) ....

unlikely (adj) ....

Chapter 5

ability (n) ....

address (v) ....

agreeably (adv) ....

anger (v) ....

background (n) ....

be quick to do sth (was – been) (phr) ....

behave (v) ....

bully (v) ....

can't be bothered (to do sth) (phr) ....

chat (v) ....

claim (v) ....

clarify (v) ....

come to sb's defence (came – come)(phr) ....

companionship (n) ....

conclude (v) ....

connections (n) ....

constant (adj) ....

courage (n) ....

curiosity (n) ....

curious (adj) ....

description (n) ....

destined (adj) ....

discovery (n) ....

disturbing (adj) ....

doubt (v) ....

dreadful (adj) ....

elegance (n) ....

expert (adj) ....

expression (n) ....

extensive (adj) ....

get away with (got – got) (phr v) ....
grand (adj) ....
greet (v) ....
head (v) ....
insistence (n) ....
intensely (adv) ....
interrupt (v) ....
joint (adj) ....
lack (v) ....
make the effort (to do sth) (made – made) (phr) ....
manage (v) ....
match (v) ....
misbehave (v) ....
mistaken (adj) ....
notion (n) ....
pale (adj) ....
parsonage (n) ....
pleasant (adj) ....
practise (v) ....
prepare oneself (phr) ....
prevent (v) ....
privilege (n) ....
progress (v) ....
proportion (n) ....
put off (put – put) (phr v) ....
quality (n) ....
reassure (v) ....
reflect (on) (v) ....
relation (n) ....
reluctant (adj) ....
remarkable (adj) ....
require (v) ....
responsibility (n) ....
retaliate (v) ....

run into (ran – run) (phr v) ....

show round (showed – shown) (phr v) ....

sickly (adj) ....

skill (n) ....

sole (adj) ....

speak well of sb (spoke – spoken) (phr) ....

stand up to sb (stood – stood) (phr v) ....

stubborn (adj) ....

unwise (adj) ....

weak (adj) ....

worsen (v) ....

Chapter 6

account (n) ....

accusation (n) ....

against all reason (phr) ....

alarmed (adj) ....

ashamed (adj) ....

assure (v) ....

attitude (n) ....

back up (phr v) ....

be in sb's best interests (was – been)(phr) ....

be up to sth (was – been) (phr) ....

become aware (became – become) (phr) ....

beyond belief (phr) ....

bold (adj) ....

catch up with (caught – caught) (phr v) ....

closeness (n) ....

compliment (n) ....

conceal (v) ....

concern (v) ....

conclusion (n) ....

consider (v) ....

damage (n) ....

deny (v) ....
develop (v) ....
dishonesty (n) ....
do everything in your power (did – done) (phr) ....
do wrong (did – done) (phr) ....
doorbell (n) ....
drawing room (n)...
elope (v) ....
entirely (adv) ....
excess (n) ....
exhausted (adj) ....
fail to do sth (phr) ....
feel sorry for sb (felt – felt) (phr) ....
feel up to sth (felt – felt) (phr v) ....
fold up (v) ....
fortune (n) ....
fully (adv)...
gain (v) ....
get one's hands on sth (got – got) (phr) ....
get the better of sb (got – got) (phr) ....
go against all reason (went – gone) (phr) ....
have no doubt (had – had) (phr) ....
high living (phr) ....
high-handed (adj) ....
hold back (held – held) (phr v) ....
hurt sb's feelings (hurt – hurt) (phr) ....
in one's best interests (phr) ....
independence (n) ....
instinctively (adv) ....
intend (v) ....
involvement (n) ....
keep sth to oneself (kept – kept) (phr) ....
laziness (n) ....
mistreat (v) ....

motive (n) ....

nonetheless (adv) ....

occur (v) ....

offend (v) ....

out of sight (phr) ....

particularly (adv) ....

passionately (adv) ....

personal (adj) ....

prejudiced (adj) ....

put an end to sth (put – put) (phr) ....

recall (v) ....

resent (v) ....

reveal (v) ....

revenge (n) ....

reward (v) ....

rudely (adv) ....

ruin (v) ....

shaken (adj) ....

shame (n) ....

sign (n) ....

silence (n) ....

social standing (phr) ....

speechless (adj) ....

stride (strode – stridden) (v) ....

struggle (v) ....

support (v) ....

suspicious (adj) ....

take up (took – taken) (phr v) ....

tend (to) (v) ....

thrust (thrust – thrust) (v) ....

unfair (adj) ....

use up (phr v) ....

win the affection of sb (won – won) (phr) ....

with the best intention (phr) ....

Chapter 7

account (n) ....

an angry word (phr) ....

as luck would have it (phr) ....

assessment (n) ....

atmosphere (n) ....

breathe a sigh of relief (phr) ....

bring sth to mind (brought – brought) (phr) ....

capable (adj) ....

chat (n) ....

commander (n) ....

concern (v) ....

conflicting (adj) ....

content (adj) ....

county (n) ....

discredit (v) ....

excitable (adj) ....

expose (v) ....

feature (n) ....

fine (adj) ....

flirt (v) ....

fraction (n) ....

generous (adj) ....

grounds (pl n) ....

grow up (grew – grown) (phr v) ....

head (for) (v) ....

housekeeper (n) ....

ill-tempered (adj) ....

imaginable (adj) ....

keep up (kept – kept) (phr v) ....

lawn (n) ....

master (n) ....

mistress (n) ....

opinion (n) ....

path (n) ....

pay a visit (paid – paid) (phr) ....

portrait (n) ....

remain (v) ....

reputation (n) ....

respect sb's wishes (phr) ....

riverbank (n) ....

sensible (adj) ....

servant (n) ....

socialise (v) ....

speak highly of sb (spoke – spoken) (phr) ....

speak up (spoke – spoken) (phr v) ....

take advantage of (took – taken) (phr) ....

take notice (took – taken) (phr)..............................

tenant (n) ....

tour (n) ....

uneasy (adj) ....

Chapter 8

accompany (v) ....

amiably (adv) ....

anxious (adj) ....

assistance (n) ....

awkward (adj) ....

bury one's face (in sth) (phr) ....

companion (n) ....

consequence (n) ....

cross (v) ....

distress (n) ....

draw a conclusion (drew – drawn) (phr)..................

equipment (n) ....

exceed one's expectations (phr) ....

extremely (adv) ....

face (v) ....
foolishness (n) ....
handkerchief (n) ....
ill temper (phr) ....
immensely (adv) ....
impress (v)..
in an attempt to (phr) ....
magnificent (adj)..
mystify (v) ....
on friendly terms (phr) ....
popularity (n) ....
puzzled (adj) ....
regret (v/n) ....
reject (v) ....
respectable (adj)...
route (n) ....
rumour (n) ....
say one's goodbyes (said – said) (phr) ....
scandal (n) ....
snub (v) ....
stressful (adj) ....
tear open (tore – torn) (phr) ....
trace (v) ....
urgent (adj) ....

Chapter 9

affair (n) ....
affectionate (adj) ....
allowance (n) ....
amount (n) ....
anew (adv) ....
appeal (n) ....
ashamed (adj) ....
attachment (n) ....

breathless (adj) ....

bring (sth) about (brought – brought) (phr v) ....

calm (v) ....

caution (v) ....

celebrate (v) ....

circumstances (pl n) ....

commit (v) ....

compassion (n)..

congratulate (v) ....

contribute (v) ....

debt (n) ....

disapproval (n) ....

drive (n) ....

drop the subject (phr) ....

due (adj) ....

elopement (n) ....

embarrassed (adj) ....

embrace (v) ....

enthusiastic (adj) ....

evidence (n) ....

faithfully (adv) ....

financial (adj) ....

fully aware (of) (phr) ....

funds (pl n) ....

gambling (n) ....

guarantee (v) ....

hopeless (adj) ....

have an effect on sb (had – had) (phr) ....

honourable (adj) ....

horrified (adj) ....

in terms of (phr) ....

increasingly (adv)..

insensitive (adj) ....

joyless (adj) ....

keep an eye on sb (kept – kept) (phr) ....

locate (v) ....

long (v) ....

make public (made – made) (phr) ....

make sense (made – made) (phr) ....

overcome (overcame – overcome) (v) ....

pay back (paid – paid) (phr v) ....

per annum (adv) ....

philosophical (adj) ....

primarily (adv) ....

provide (v) ....

pull up (phr v) ....

put down (put – put) (phr v) ....

reaction (n) ....

repay (repaid – repaid) (v) ....

settle (v) ....

share (n) ....

shortly (adv) ....

sincerely (adv) ....

stand firm (stood – stood) (phr) ....

stray (v) ....

swallow your pride (phr) ....

terms (pl n) ....

to an extent (phr) ....

transfer (v) ....

trivial (adj) ....

unaware (adj) ....

unmoved (adj) ....

willingly (adv) ....

with curiosity (phr) ....

worthlessness (n) ....

Chapter 10

anticipate (v) ....

background (n) ....

be out of your senses (was – been) (phr) ....

betray (v) ....

carriage (n) ....

charming (adj) ....

considerably (adv) ....

debt of gratitude (phr) ....

declare (v) ....

delighted (adj) ....

deserve (v) ....

deserving (adj) ....

disapproving (adj) ....

dismount (v) ....

distressed (adj) ....

drift (away) (v) ....

extraordinary (adj) ....

form (v) ....

frustrating (adj) ....

Good gracious! (phr) ....

gradually (adv) ....

gratitude (n) ....

have an interest in (had – had) (phr) ....

have no trouble doing sth (had – had) (phr) ....

headstrong (adj) ....

in contrast (phr) ....

in return (phr) ....

incredibly (adv) ....

instruction (n) ....

insult (v) ....

judgement (n) ....

make (sth) of (sb/sth) (made – made) (phr v) ....

match (n) ....

noble (adj) ....

obey (v) ....

optimism (n) ....

part with (phr v) ....

pause (n) ....

peculiar (adj) ....

plainly (adv) ....

principle (n) ....

reasonable (adj) ....

reconsider (v) ....

relieve (v) ....

remark (v) ....

sb's affections (phr) ....

scornfully (adv) ....

self-importance (n) ....

shooting season (phr) ....

silence (v) ....

stylish (adj) ....

suitable (adj) ....

suppose (v) ....

teach sb a lesson (taught – taught) (phr) ....

tell sb sth to their face (told – told) (phr) ....

unchanged (adj) ....

undergo (underwent – undergone) (v) ....

voice (v) ....

worthy (adj) ....